MODERN DIPLOMACY

Uwem Essia

The BRICS and Multilateral Diplomacy

TABLE OF CONTENT

TABLE OF CONTENT ii

INTRODUCTION 1

CHAPTER ONE: THE BRICS COALITION AS A GLOBAL DISRUPTION 5

Disruption, Disruptive Innovational Thinking, and Design Thinking 5

Top-Down or Bottom-Up Approach 12

Disruption Innovation Modeling Applied to the BRICS de-dollarization Initiative 13

Disruptive versus sustaining innovation 24

Disruption is a process 25

CHAPTER TWO: BRICS – A SUCCESSFUL MARRIAGE OF STRANGE BEDFELLOW 33

Lessons from the BRICS Coalition Experience 47

CHAPTER THREE: MANAGING DIVERGENT PERSPECTIVES – THE BRICS EXPERIENCE 51

Multilateralism as the Cornerstone of a Multipolar World 53

The case between multilateralism and unilateralism 56

BRICS and negotiating fair global governance in a "post-American world order" 58

CHAPTER FOUR: DESIGNING A VIABLE PATHWAY TO DE-DOLLARIZATION 64

Develop alternative institutions and markets and support far-reaching system reforms 69

Using a go-it-alone strategy alone 72

Using Negotiations Alone......73

Expressions of the U.S. Dollar Dominant Currency Status. 74

The BRICS Strategic Attack on the U.S. Dollar......75

The BRICS De-dollarization Initiative......78

CHAPTER FIVE: COLLECTIVE MOBILIZATION FOR DE-DOLLARIZATION 80

BRICS as a Financial Coalition 81

The Pandemic Induced De-Dollarization Commitments.... 84

The Gradual Rise of BRICS Members' Currencies 86

The BRICS Case for Reserve Currency Diversification 89

CHAPTER SIX: THE BRICS INSTITUTIONS AND MARKET MECHANISMS 106

The NDB and De-dollarizing Development of Finance 107

The Yuan Oil Futures and De-dollarizing Global Oil Trade
......115

Escalation of the US-China Trade War 118

CHAPTER SEVEN: BRICS GLOBAL FINANCIAL INFRASTRUCTURE 124

China's SWIFT Alternative......128

Russia SWIFT Alternative......134

"China-Russia Plus" Coalition to Create a SWIFT Alternative
......138

CHAPTER EIGHT: A COMMON BRICS PAYMENT SYSTEM AND DIGITAL CURRENCY 142

Using Blockchain Technology to Build a BRICS Digital Currency 145

BRICS Plus: De-dollarization Mobilization beyond BRICS 152

CHAPTER NINE: NEGOTIATING FOR REFORMS OF THE EXISTING SYSTEM **162**

Reforming the Global Reserve Currency Structure 169

Weakening the Dollar's Dominance as the Vehicle Currency in Trade 173

Disrupting the Dollar's Dominance in Global Equity Markets 180

CHAPTER TEN: EVOLUTION OF BRICS AS A DE-DOLLARIZATION COALITION **186**

CHAPTER ELEVEN: A NEW GLOBAL CURRENCY – THE CHALLENGE OF COORDINATION **198**

A BRICS Alternative to the U.S. Dollar is Being Over-ambitious 200

The BRIC Commodity/Currency Swap Proposal is possible 204

Ramp up BRICS Productivity before considering a Global Currency 207

Other reserve currencies will naturally evolve over time 209

De-dollarization initiatives can't displace the US dollar's global reserve currency status 212

The U.S. has a responsibility to adjust in line with changing realities 215

CONCLUSION **219**

The desperation of Russia for de-dollarization is understandable 223

The BRICS coalition needs more time to prepare for a common currency 224

SOURCES **227**

INTRODUCTION

The BRICS is a coalition of strange bedfellows. It differs generally from the common model of association among countries often based either on geographical proximity, ideology, or similarity in some social, political, and cultural traits. The BRICS coalition transformed from an idea mooted by Goldman Sachs O'Neil, that a set of four fast-growing countries – Brazil, Russia, India, and China – will dominate the world economy by 2050, to a real coalition of those countries. The manifestation of what is commonly described as the BRICS thesis demonstrates the power of ideas, and the fact that a group of entities having a common interest and a shared vision can work together. In other words, birds of different feathers can fly together and the different sounds created by the movement of their diverse feathers can produce a piece of beautiful melodic music.

Multilateral diplomacy helps entities in a group to identify their common vision and amalgamate their activities in ways that aid them work together regardless of differences in geopolitical, economic, and sociocultural backgrounds. In modern diplomacy, there are no permanent friends or enemies, but common interests. Even countries at war can still find common grounds for agreement. The BRICS bloc has demonstrated that the diversity of members of a bloc or coalition should not inhibit the group's effective functioning. On the contrary greater diversity help identify the necessary complementarities needed for gainful exchange among the group members.

This book explains how the soft power of the BRICS members is agglomerating to keep the bloc stronger and why their diversity makes augmenting their capabilities more successful. Thus, what matters most in modern diplomacy is the commonality of interests and goals, augmentation can take care of any missing factor. It follows that very different nations can come together to function effectively as a diplomatic bloc. It is indeed easier for countries with similar histories, and geographical closeness to work against each other. The relationship between African countries demonstrates this. For instance, it is easier and sometimes cheaper to travel to Dubai from Nigeria, than from Nigeria to Cameroon, although both countries have several things in common. So, what matters more is common interests and goals, and a shared vision.

The BRICS bloc has so far used augmentation to nurture a formidable financial-economic bloc that is being embraced by regional and non-regional allies of the member states, thereby helping to extend the soft power dispersion of the bloc globally. Moreover, the fact that the BRICS contains both developing and developed nations, as well as communist and democratic nations, renders it more appealing to groupings of countries that share each of these characteristics and promotes a pitch toward non-capitalist nations in transition as well as toward developed nations. Progressively, the BRICS alliances will help pull countries aware of the unhealthy extremist tendencies to a blended, middle path, political economic cum governance milieu where it becomes difficult to classify countries as capitalist, communist, authoritarian, or libertarian because the best features of all ideological sides will ultimately dissolve and get blended in the BRICS melting pot.

CHAPTER ONE: THE BRICS COALITION AS A GLOBAL DISRUPTION

Disruption, Disruptive Innovational Thinking, and Design Thinking

Disruption modeling is recurrently discussed in the business economics literature. The aspects commonly discussed include disruption business models, disruptive innovations, development disruptions, IT disruptions, etc. The common view is that an entity (singularly or a coalition) can use disruption as a tool to have a competitive edge over its rivals. Disruption innovation thinking allows a progressive entity to think in terms of identifying possible events that could disruptions in the future and take steps to preempt and benefit from them rather than just watch them happen. The BRICs thesis propounded by Goldman Sachs' O'Neil that the 4 BRICs economies will become the fastest growing economies of the world by 2050 was disruption thinking. And the effort by the BRICS countries to actualize the thesis with deliberate plans and programs is disrupting innovational thinking.

Design thinking is the process of creating designs to demonstrate that the desired outcomes are achievable. In other words, design thinking helps to fill the space between where we are now and where we want to be, by demonstrating where we ought to be graphically and rendering it attractive enough to motivate the responsible actors to prioritize taking steps to actualize it. What connects disruption, disruptive innovational thinking, and design thinking is the fact of uncertainty. In a highly uncertain world, changes come so fast that no one can claim to have firm control over any situation. Doing nothing may be considered worse than doing the wrong thing. But it is necessary to gather and analyze the necessary information continually for insight on which course of action to take. At the same time, most decisions must be taken very quickly which makes planning difficult. So, the capacity to think strategically is important. In a highly disruptive environment, as we have now, having the appropriate capacities and tools for identifying vulnerabilities and threats, and dealing with them preemptively can help entities prevent several adversities and turn some misfortunes into opportunities. This in simple terms is the essence of disruptive innovational thinking. The key points linked disruption

a. *Disrupt or be disrupted*

The quote "disrupt or be disrupted" is commonly cited as coming from Silicon Valley. Business success today is more about searching for opportunities/niches to out-compete others. Competition is inevitably disruptive for all entities, including countries. You have to self-disrupt to move faster. A winner today must continue to self-disrupt to remain on top. The losers self-disrupt to become winners. The business world thus advances from one station of disruption to another. Factors external to markets create their share of disruptions. For instance, tsunamis, pandemics, and terrorist attacks happen. A sudden invasion of one country by another can cause markets to crash. Preparedness and resiliency are needed. Entities also require measures to help them build immunity for sundry disruptions.

b. Focusing on the customer

Disruption models pay attention to the target customers and their needs. Disruptors aim to solve the customer's problem and earn from doing so. Sound disruption models are thus pragmatic and situation-sensitive. Being customer focused implies that disruption models should be flexible and able to adjust to changing customer needs. The disruptor's challenge is heightened by the fact that customers typically know when they are satisfied, but are often unable to say exactly how, when, and where the satisfaction is created. So, the disruptor has to use design thinking to demonstrate to the customer what he needs as distinct from what he may be offered currently in the market. Design thinking helps the disruptor move steps ahead of the customer and market to discover how to continually make things easier for the customers, and capture their loyalty. The disruptor-innovator whether a single entity or a coalition needs a strategic business model to demonstrate to the customers how the innovation works. As the customers experience the new offer, and find it better at servicing their needs, it is expected that they switch from what is offered by the incumbent to what the disruptor-innovator offers. The niche of the disruptor-innovator is to add value to the customers' experience either for the same or at a lower cost. The disrupter-innovator wins new customers and market shares by solving some problems for customers. This is how disruption facilitates competition and business growth now. Used together, disruption, disruption modeling, and design thinking helps the innovator-disruptors (or the newcomer) to change the market behavior of the customers and win them over from the incumbent who has been dominating the market for a long time.

c. Why Disruptive Innovational Thinking is Necessary

Today's customers are continually in search of solutions that make them better off in terms of value for money, benefits received, convenience, and timeliness of delivery. Disruptor-innovators attract and retain customers by continually showing that they are understood and served better. Successful disruptor-innovators construct or adopt models that balance internal and external concerns simultaneously, with the right mix of innovative products and innovative business models, to deliver disruptive innovation solutions to an existing market. How successful an innovator-disruptor is will depend on how well the unmet needs are identified and the disruption models designed to address them. An unmet need can either be a low-end or high-end repressed demand. The low end supports the price-sensitive customers, while the more premium customers are at the high end.

Top-Down or Bottom-Up Approach

The disruptor-innovator may decide to enter the market from the top, by producing straight ahead for premium customers. Otherwise, they enter from the bottom by producing first the cheaper goods for ordinary or low-income customers. Or they can have a two-way entry point by producing top-down and bottom-top goods/services simultaneously. The most famous example of top-down disruption is Apple. They started by making computers for rich people who could afford to pay a lot of money for them. But later they made the iPod, which was a lot cheaper and more accessible to everyone. And thereafter they make the iPhone, which is also targeted at premium clients but slowly offering also other offerings for a broader mass. The most famous example of bottom-up disruption is Walmart. They came into the market by offering products that were cheaper than what people were used to paying. And focus on offering cheaper prices, to take over huge market shares and become the biggest retail corporation globally. Typically, a successful business model consists of various elements and combines different income streams. It is difficult to say which model is better. It depends on one's preferences, goals, and capabilities.

Disruption Innovation Modeling Applied to the BRICS de-dollarization Initiative

Disruptive innovation modeling is influenced by competition and the incorporation of an increasing arrear of predictive tools and methods, such as scenario analysis, simulation, actor analysis, etc. Disruptive innovation modeling is used as a powerful set of tools to support innovation-led growth.

a. Who is a disruptor-innovator?

A disruptor-innovator is a less-known, less-equipped rival who is seeking to overtake a better-known or entrenched incumbent or defender who is desirous to retain his advantageous position. In our present context, the BRICS coalition is the disruptor-innovator while the incumbent is the U.S. and its U.S. dollar whose exorbitant privilege the U.S. enjoys. The success factor for the disruptor-innovator is the ability to maintain a track record of consistency and integrate insights gathered continually from research and experience into the original framework. Doing so is necessary because everything keeps changing quickly. A winning disruptor-innovator has to be situationally agile and readily adaptable to innovations as they spring up.

b. *Information on the Needs of Customers is Important*

Customer relations is an important source of information for driving change. The customers, in this case, are the investors, central banks' officials, trade and investment experts, policymakers of countries, etc. It follows that to succeed in its de-dollarization initiative, the BRICS coalition must put in place a research unit that can continually collect timely information on the needs of investors, central banks, and foreign exchange dealers among other identified actors and interest parties to identify the difficulties they are having with the current dollar-dominated system and what changes are required to have a better, easier, cost-effective, and more rewarding experience. Taking incremental steps to ensure that the NDB, CRA, and the BRICS countries offer its clients better experiences than what is offered by the incumbent institutions can go a long way to effecting the necessary change over time.

Quite often, the disruptor-innovator, like the BRICS coalition, is a smaller entity with fewer resources but sets out to challenge and surpass an established incumbent or more advanced entity. An incumbent is often the resource-rich player, like the U.S. who having operated for a longer time has substantial scale economies to benefit from. Most incumbents are focused on the niches they already built. They are comfortable innovating or improving along existing technological and market trajectories. They continue to offer services for their traditional customers. With the established markets at their disposal, the incumbents can readily ignore the continuing changes in customer preferences and possible growth in the number of upcoming customer segments that seek more convenient and or cheaper serving options. This is possible since from the behavioral economic perspective, the customer is mindful of loss aversion and has status quo bias and so would easily stick to what he already knows to avoid the risk of making unnecessary losses. Accordingly, the customer is likely to continue patronizing what he is used to (the U.S dollar as reserve currency, medium of exchange in international trade, and dollar bonds) until it is sufficiently demonstrated to him (by the BRICS coalition de-dollarization initiative) that there are suitable and viable alternatives to what the incumbent (U.S. dollar-dominated system) offers. A disruptor-innovator that is researching continually can incrementally displace the incumbent by focusing on making incremental small changes because the incumbent may rarely get so close to the customers to understand their current discomfort and what their present needs are.

The strength of a disruptor-innovator is how well he can investigate and understand the gaps that need to be filled to have a customer satisfied and his effectiveness in designing innovations to make the customers more satisfied. Also, a winning disruptor-innovator can target the overlooked segments or ignored customer needs, and by so doing gain a foothold by offering more suitable or functional offers often at lower prices. Thus, while incumbents are preoccupied with established niches, and often have little time left to look beyond their sphere of influence, the disruptor-innovator shines his eyes in search of novelties to offer the customers. The easiest way that the disruptor-innovator can leapfrog to leadership and compete favorably with the incumbent is to solve a problem that the incumbent may have taken for granted.

The disruptor-innovator can focus on solving problems for those at the bottom. For the BRICS coalition, this may involve creating club good (like concessional loans for poor countries). They can simultaneously also create dedicated club good for advanced countries (like making BRICS member bonds more attractive for investors from the advanced countries). From the lowest and highest points, extending the club goods to the rest of the customer groups is easy if the experience of the early starters is considered worthwhile. Disruption occurs when mainstream customers start adopting the BRICS club goods.

c. The BRICS coalition will do better if the focus on the markets that the incumbent overlooks

The BRICS coalition can leapfrog to leadership if the focus in markets that the incumbent overlooks. The incumbent often pays more attention to his most profitable and demanding customer segments by offering them innovative products. Quite often little attention is paid to those considered as less important, or yet-to-emerge customer segments.

A practical example can be used to illustrate this. The U.S. dollar-dominated system of the World Bank, IMF, and the Overseas Development Assistance (ODA) focus on giving loans and aid to the governments of the less developed countries without considering the weak absorptive capacities of those countries. In nearly all cases while substantial debts are accumulated, very little development takes place because the funds are misappropriated and or embezzled. The BRICS coalition can act differently in the interest of the ignored population of these countries by setting up global corporations to directly implement the projects and institute the appropriate cost recovery mechanisms and processes. For instance, assume that the Nigerian government seeks a loan to build railway lines to connect the major cities in the country. Upon approval of such a loan, the BRICS coalition can create an infrastructure development corporation as a special purpose vehicle (SPV) to directly engage contractors for the execution of the project and monitor the same to ensure timely completion and value-for-money in terms of quality standard and project scope. The project execution protocol has to include a cost recovery system to ensure loan repayment over a given payback period.

Note that the current (incumbent) system takes for granted that governments will use the loans/aid judiciously which is not true. If the BRICS coalition implements its projects this way, especially in the less developed countries, the capital project implementation rate will improve significantly, the population will enjoy more developed infrastructure, corruption will reduce, and more importantly, the BRIC club good will win the hearts and minds of the population in the countries where such projects are implemented.

d. The BRICS coalition will leapfrog to leadership by creating new market footholds

The disruptor-innovator gains a faster and deeper market penetration when he succeeds to create new-market footholds. This can be achieved by creating markets whose potential existed but was never exploited. Or he can turn some non-customers into customers. A disruptive innovation can start from one of such footholds to make its mark. The disruptor-innovator does not necessarily need to catch up with mainstream customers of the incumbent at the beginning but will do so as the quality of his offers grows and surpasses the industry's best practice standards.

For example, the NDB can have a special program for extending long-term credit to major private firms investing in capital-intensive sectors like power, urban water supply, petroleum refining, optic fiber connection, etc. Currently, the World Bank lends to governments. But the governments in most less developed countries will rarely invest in these capital-intensive projects. Lending directly to the major private investors (and consortiums) with proven track record of performance can create a new market niche that were hitherto ignored.

Disruptive versus sustaining innovation

The incumbents are more interested in sustaining innovations than they are in disruptive innovations. Sustaining innovations generally aim to make things better in the eyes of an incumbent's existing customers. Sustaining innovations rarely aim to make new products, but rather aim to provide better offers of the same product. Reducing the cost and time spent to complete a SWIFT transaction is an example of sustaining innovation. But having an alternative SWIFT that eliminated the use of domiciliary (or foreign currency accounts) so that Indians and Brazilians can for instance transfer the equivalent values of rupees in the Brazilian reais directly to their bank accounts in their respective countries directly is a disruptive innovation.

Disruptive innovations may initially be considered inferior and few incumbent customers may be willing to switch to the new offering. But the situation changes as quality rises enough to satisfy them. Once that happened, they adopt the new product and happily accept its lower price. This is how disruption drives prices down in a market. However, since both sustaining and disruptive innovations lead to increased efficiency and may result in new products/services being created, distinguishing them is sometimes tricky.

Disruption is a process

Disruptive innovation is not a product or service. It is a process. It refers to the process by which products/services evolve. A product/service is disruptive when it is quantum leaped from the fringe to the mainstream. Since disruptive innovation takes time to manifest, it is easily overlooked by incumbents. The disruptor-innovator focuses first on getting the business model right, before considering the disruption good or product. When he succeeds, their movement from the fringe (the low end of the market or a new market) to the mainstream erodes first the incumbents' market share and then their profitability. But it must be considered that the incumbent may get quite creative in the defense of his established markets. Hence complete substitution, if it ever happens at all, may take decades, because the incremental profit from staying with the old model can keep the incumbent still at the top. The fact that disruption can take time helps to protect the disruptors from being fought too early by the incumbents and gives them time to continue cutting from beneath.

a. The Disruptor-Innovator Must Adopt Smart Models

Winning disruptor-innovators adopt business models that are flexible, pragmatic, and able to deal more effectively with the problem at hand. This is possible because the star disruptor-innovator pays attention to research and scenario analysis to forecast and study future trends.

b. Disruptive innovation has a risk of failure

A disruptor-innovator has to accept that there is a risk of failure. But his commitment to continuing research eases the process by which a particular failure can be re-engineered into a new opportunity. Success is not built into the definition of disruption. Some disruptive paths may lead to failure. But failures is not an evidence of the deficiencies of disruption theory; they are simply boundary markers for the theory's application. Besides, all failures offer learning opportunities.

c. Disruptions should be hurried – they should be allowed to flow naturally

Disruption should be allowed to happen naturally at its pace and not forced. The BRICS coalition should not aim to achieve total de-dollarization overnight. Efforts should be put into building the internal research, policy, and implementation structures of the BRICS and getting them continually adjusted as it becomes needful. It does not call for sweeping or wholesale changes in the structure of the organization. A new division to focus solely on emerging growth opportunities that arise from a disruption should be considered. At the same time, however, disruptive innovation has to be deliberate. Little incremental actions in the right direction are very helpful, and some direct and or indirect efforts are required. As noted earlier ongoing research efforts are essential. Customers want to be happy and satisfied but many of them do not know how to achieve it. Many customers are victims of media manipulation, peer pressure, and public opinion. Few customers can say what they need to do to achieve what they want. Hence the sweeping assumption in economic theory that consumers have full knowledge of what they want is at best half-truth. With proper design thinking and effective communication, a disruptor-innovator can sway the thinking of customers towards preferring a particular new product. What is important is learning about opportunities that the current market players have been ignoring and designing solutions that the customer finds attractive to accept. Once the design is done, a business model is needed to place the innovation within the reach of the customers.

d. Disruptor-innovator takes advantage of repressed market demands

The star disruptor-innovator takes advantage of unmet needs. Repressed market demands are the need of the consumers that are currently met with products/services they are not fully satisfied with or products lacking the features to make the consumer's life easier.

e. Disruptor-innovator makes ongoing innovation a necessity

Innovation that offers better opportunities at a reasonable cost is the foundation for disruptive business modeling. Winning disrupters do not necessarily need to reinvent the wheel. It is sufficient to settle on solving simple problems of customers at the beginning. With time, doing so can add up to bigger market effects. Once there is a strong will to solve problems and create new demands in the process the stage for disruption is set. Furthermore, a disrupter needs to consider the following seriously:

- Find opportunities in the existing markets to carve a niche.

- Nurture ideas that make the use of some existing products more rewarding or easier.

- Deliver innovations that make the product cheaper or more affordable for the customers.

- Reduce the distribution chain and throw some intermediaries out of business so consumer surplus increases. And,

- Adapt to changes in consumer behavior.

CHAPTER TWO: BRICS – A SUCCESSFUL MARRIAGE OF STRANGE BEDFELLOW

The BRICS is indeed a coalition of strange bedfellows. The bloc differs generally from the norms of association among countries, which are commonly on the basis of geographical proximity, ideology, or similarity in other social, political, cultural, or historical traits. BRIC is originally an idea mooted by Goldman Sachs O'Neil to forecast describe the growth prospect of a set of four fast-growing countries. Basically, O'Neil's report forecasted that by 2050, Brazil, Russia, India, and China would together become the most dominant economies of the world based on their growth projections. Thereafter the

BRICS members pulled together and adopted actualizing O'Neil's thesis as their common goal beginning from 2009, and currently they have become a formidable force. This manifestation of what is the BRICs thesis has demonstrated that ideas are powerful, and also that with a common interest and shared vision, 'birds of different feathers can fly together', and the different sound created by the varying movement of their feathers can produce a piece of delightful melodic music.

Multilateral diplomacy can help entities identify a common vision and amalgamate their activities in ways that help them work together regardless of their different geopolitical, economic, and sociocultural backgrounds. Note that in modern diplomacy, there are no permanent friends or enemies, but common interests. Even countries at war can still find common grounds for agreement. The BRICS bloc has demonstrated that the diversity of members may not necessarily inhibit the effectiveness of coalitions. On the contrary greater diversity can nurture and grow the complementarities needed for gainful exchange among group members.

The key to keeping the members together despite their difference is the process of augmentation. This involves the agglomeration of the soft power of the BRICS members to fill identified gaps. And diversity of the members makes soft power augmentation more successful, and in many instances turn differences among the members of the bloc into a strength. This confirms that what matters most in modern diplomacy is the commonality of interests and goals, and not necessarily geographical, ideological, cultural-linguistic, or any other form of historical affinities. Once a group can identify a shared interest that is not dependent on the particular character of each nation (political, social, economic), as they come together, it is possible to create a process of functional "non-differentiation" or melting pot mechanisms within the bloc to match the weaknesses of some members with the strengths of the others, and by so doing countries with varying capacities and capabilities can grow together within a multilateral diplomatic bloc.

Aside from being distantly located and having remarkably political, economic, and social differences, the BRICS countries differ as well in terms of their respective soft power profiles. Brazil's soft power emanates from its history of minimal armed conflicts (so far non-possession of WMD), and enjoying active membership in several multilateral organizations. South Africa prides itself on having one of the most liberal constitutions in the world. Like Brazil, South Africa has extensive multilateral engagement and can be described as an important soft power broker on the global stage. India's soft power is cultural and political: an epic culture and a site of four religions; Bollywood is the largest filmmaking destination in the world; and its diaspora population is well supported by the government. India is also the world's most stable democracy in a nation that is ethnically and politically fractured. China's "charm offensive" covers everything from globally promoting Confucian thought to building networks of friendship with African nations from whom it imports raw materials. China is also able to connect its soft power purposefully with its hard power initiative. The Sun Zi (Art of War) dualism of "zheng" (direct means) and "qi" (indirect means) represents opposing strategies that synthesize into a strategy of smart or cosmopolitan power. Hence for the Chinese, the hard and soft power are located together.

China envisions its soft power initiative as principally spearheaded by an ideological offensive, hence the proliferation of Confucian Institutes throughout the world to among other things fill the void left by the ideological decline of Communism. Promoting Confucian values (which stress the roles of family, obedience, and authority) gives the CPC significant ideological (spiritual) support.

Russia and China have much in common. Like Chinese leaders, Russian leaders have underscored the importance of soft power in their foreign policy. Much of this soft power offensive has been to compete with Western soft power and deliver a superpower image akin to that of the U.S. The Russian state has engineered many institutions and initiatives that make Russian society more visible to the world; such as, the international TV station *Russia Today*; mega events like the Sochi Olympics in 2014; and the hosting of the World Cup in 2018. Russia has also made significant efforts at regional soft power dispersion through the Russotrudnichestvo, an agency dedicated to enhancing endearment from 125 million ethnic Russians and Russian-speaking people residing in the former USSR.

The diversity and geographic spread of the BRICS, summarily described above, extends the scope for soft power augmentation among the members. It is much easier for countries with similar histories, and geographical closeness to work against the influence of the members. Several examples in the African continent demonstrate this. It is easier and cheaper to travel to Dubai from most African countries than to travel from one African country to another. Yet many African countries have several attributes in common. For the BRICS members, augmentation has helped fill gaps and nurtured an amiable bloc that is widely embraced by the regional and non-regional allies of the members, which further extends the soft power dispersion globally.

Also, the fact that the BRICS contains both developing and developed nations, as well as communist and democratic nations, renders it more appealing to groupings of countries that share at least one of the characteristics. This promotes a pitch toward non-capitalist nations in transition as well as toward developed nations. Progressively, the BRICS alliances will help pull all countries aware of extreme views to a blended political economic and governance milieu where it becomes difficult to classify countries as capitalist, communist, authoritarian, or libertarian. This is particularly so as the BRICS disassociates itself from any specific military objectives aside from promoting international security.

The non-additivity aspect of soft power dispersion from augmentation manifests itself in several ways. The membership mix creates ample opportunities for complementarities so that soft power arsenals are far more complete through amalgamation in a bloc. Each member brings a soft power profile that can serve to complete the profiles of other nations. Admiration of the great superpowers Russia and China mixes nicely with the endearing empathy that India and Brazil garner from their developing democratic status. The traditional great civilizations of India, Russia, and China nicely complement the positive ingénue effects of Brazil and South Africa as young nations. In this respect, the BRICS generates admiration for polar opposite soft traits. Additionally, the admiration that Brazil and South Africa attain by becoming role models of domestic democratic practices and values complements the international charm offensive of China. The manifold possibilities for complementarities with and between both domestic and international components of soft power are enormous.

But complementarities go beyond traits and show themselves in other ways. There is also temporal complementarity, for which diversity of membership is especially fortuitous for the bloc. Soft power profiles vary according to current policies and outcomes. At times specific nations may find their soft power waning (such as Russia and China at present, due to territorial disputes), but it is unlikely that the changes in soft power will be perfectly correlated, especially among a group as diverse as the BRICS. The more positive images of present domestic politics in South Africa and India serve as temporal counterweights to Russia and China's regional disputes and authoritarian regimes. In terms of financial portfolio theory, the best possible combination of risk and return on investments occurs when portfolios are composed of very different types of assets (i.e., extensive diversification is always best). Similarly, a diverse bloc such as the BRICS offers the best complementary mix of soft power profiles: their images are less likely to be correlated due to completely different geo-political environments.

Beyond the important diplomatic statements that emanate from the meetings of the BRICS, the bloc's creation of the New Development Bank (NDB) and the Contingency Reserve Fund (CRF) in 2014 has generated an institutional manifestation of soft power. While the capitalization of the two, although significant at one billion dollars each, is still modest compared to the World Bank and IMF, the creation of development lending institutions outside of Western purview has served to reinforce a normative paradigm shift.

While there will be some overlap in lending procedures, the NDB is not devoted to the politics or the economic models of the West in issuing or supervising infrastructural lending. Similarly, the CRF's governing principles reflect little of the Washington consensus, which suggests rigid management of short-term balance of payments relief. The guiding principles of these two institutions embrace a model of lending that is far more South-friendly and consequently opposed to idiosyncrasies of the Western model which undergirds the IMF and World Bank.

The BRICS Strategy for Economic Partnership (2015) also nicely reflects how disparate and diverse actors can consolidate efforts to build a global power bloc. The Partnership aspires to a single bloc presence that generates diplomatic and economic weight on the global scene. It is envisioned as working through extensive initiatives that coordinate policies and interests across both state and non-state actors. The document announcing the partnership mirrors an insightful view into the process of compounding power among disparate nations. The collective goals place large international issues in the purview of the bloc, particularly development, free trade, financial transparency, sustainable growth, poverty relief, human rights, and health. Thus, the bloc is making the business of the larger global community its own business and entrenching it firmly as a key diplomatic force in the wider global discourse.

The BRICS bloc is emerging as a leader in throwing open discussions on several international issues, like international financial regulation, IFI management, pushing regional solutions to global problems, trade, development programs, food security, and the environment. This has connected the BRICS to various regional groups and is manifesting in several countries in the developed and developing world seeking to participate in its governmental and non-governmental fora: informal meetings, Sherpa meetings, research centers, seminars, think tank symposia, business forums, law forums, statistical cooperation, cultural forums, and greater cooperation in sports. Also, the strategy adopted by the BRICS underscores cooperation in energy, agriculture, innovation, and natural resource production. Hence the bloc assumes a greater ability to marshal diplomatic power as a result of collective influence in these four areas. On a more regionally focused issue, the bloc initiative on solving the problem of political instability in the Middle East and North Africa has also demonstrated the power of amalgamative involvement in crucial international issues.

Lessons from the BRICS Coalition Experience

The BRICS experience so far generates important lessons for nations that are seeking to leverage their power through amalgamation in international blocs or organizations. The lessons are summarized below.

a. In modern diplomacy, unlike terms attract and stick better than like terms

Opposite can attract. It follows that with proper diplomacy a protracted violent conflict such as between Palestinians and Israelis can be resolved and the two sides live together. Once it is possible to identify their common interest, then it will be possible to build some shared goals and vision around it. Nations should explore possibilities for collective power through diversity. Regional proximity and domestic similarities may limit the reach of the organization's nations build. If nations think of wider representation and complementarities, rather than the need to replicate themselves in blocs, the resulting associations may make a far greater diplomatic impact. You don't need common nations to promote cooperation, only common interests.

b. Less barriers against friendship and accommodation makes bonding with countries easier and more rewarding

Bad fences make good neighbors. The BRICS have demonstrated that lowering barriers against friendship and accommodation among heretofore unaligned or marginally aligned nations can raise the individual and collective power of the bloc members significantly. In today's globalized world nations can't successfully shut their doors against others. If you restrict the importation of what your citizens need so much, they will find ways to smuggle them in. If you repress them excessively, then be prepared for a revolt someday soon. Wise leaders endeavor to give their citizens reasonable measure of freedom.

c. Be willing to support group members in times of need for possible reciprocation

Be as much as possible generous without being unnecessarily critical of the positions of other countries. This will increase friendships and reduce strained relationships significantly. Nations that have experienced strained relations can't effectively work together in common ventures. And difficult countries may lose opportunities in the future. The BRICS have served to provide a venue of proximity through which nations can leverage new and stronger bonds while abating tense issues that have heretofore served as diplomatic roadblocks. Finally, don't judge a bloc by its members. The BRICS have shown that a bloc is more than an additive function.

CHAPTER THREE: MANAGING DIVERGENT PERSPECTIVES – THE BRICS EXPERIENCE

The establishment of the BRICS was hailed by the coalition members and observers as the rise of a countervailing force to the Western development agenda. The expectation was that Russia and China would lead the organization by leveraging their advanced economies to the benefit of other members. Western countries frequently express concern about how BRICS could affect Africa's trade with the EU and the U.S. The BRICS members have diverging interests, with some countries in open conflict with each other. China and India's regional conflict is weighing heavily on the organization, and meaningful economic cooperation involving the two powers appears difficult but is happening. There is also little support for Russia to be had from New Delhi, with Prime Minister Narendra Modi declaring that "this is not the time for war"; pointing to the fact that the Russian-Ukrainian war may pose a challenge to Russia reaping fuller gains from the coalition.

China needs a stable market for its goods, and BRICS members alone can't offer such demand. What Beijing wants is further access to Western markets and consumers on terms that are more favorable to her. China may thus be seeing the BRICS as a stepping stone to global economic dominance. China understands that it is costly for her to take over global leadership role from the U.S. Hence China is not desiring an alternative to the Western-dominated global trade regime, but it rather seeks to upstage the West and control the existing global economic order. Through BRICS, South Africa, and Brazil were hoping to gain access to global markets and grow their economies, and not take sides in conflicts caused by China and Russia.

Multilateralism as the Cornerstone of a Multipolar World

Multilateralism has become the cornerstone of an emerging multipolar world, where the BRICS coalition will play a major role. The bloc emerges as a concrete multilateral group that seeks to reshape the contours of the international system that appears to have denied the BRICS members a place in the hierarchy of global powers. The BRICS bloc has the potential to become the world's voice for the states of the global South. In its brief period of existence, the BRICS has expanded its diplomatic role rapidly and is advocating for a larger voice both in the sphere of economics as well as security forums. The bloc emerged as a platform for the call to reform the international order. It seeks to achieve this at three key levels: at the member country level by the leaders member states voicing the need to change at global forums; within the BRICS coalition by the members demonstrating the world they seek through how they relate among themselves; and by the BRICS organization creating and sustaining new institutions like the NDB. It has become obvious that the BRICS bloc seeks to reshape the international system and the process of global governance through the process of multilateral diplomacy. The process of globalization with its economic and regional integration necessitated the rapid growth of multilateral diplomacy at the regional level to fulfill its functions at that level. BRICS converted from an idea into an institution, by the nations concerned, with the meeting of foreign ministers held, on the margins of a Group of 8 meetings, between Brazil, China, Russia, and India in St. Petersburg in 2008. It emerged as a potential bloc to primarily counterbalance the developed world vis-à-vis the emerging nations.

The financial crises of 2008 and the resilience which the member states of the BRICs nation displayed was the rallying point for the institutionalized cooperation among them. The legitimacy crisis that was caused by the international financial order led to cooperation among this group of emerging powers that were relatively stable on the economic front. The trust that developed among them in the financial area finally led to a spillover effect, with the BRICS nations further developing cooperation in broader areas though the root cause of their emergence has gradually disappeared. International politics, cooperation, and conflict among the member states are also impacting the aspect of global governance and thus form a crucial part of the study of BRICS.

The case between multilateralism and unilateralism

BRICS as an organization has its growth, both individually as well as jointly. This growth is undeterred by the U.S.' stand to remain a unilateral power. But the success of the BRICS over a short period indicates that multipolarity is an inevitable growth of this present world system. BRICS as an organization signifies a unified version of multipolarity. Multilateralism enhances unity in diversity. However, bloc can become and continue to grow as an influential force in the global economic power equation without being hegemonic or needing to challenge the U.S. The BRICS will continue to be relevant in its own right in the international sphere despite the differences among the member countries. It will continue to remain as a coalition of emerging nations that challenge the discourse dominated by the West and also successfully provide an alternative idea of the aspect of global governance. The bloc primarily emerged as a potential unit to counterbalance the policies of the developed states. In a multipolar world order, it has gradually evolved into a significant coalition. Since it evolved incrementally into a forum that is more comprehensive and one that holds dialogue on diverse issues, thus it can be regarded as a multilateral forum.

China seeks to nurture an environment of cooperative nature through BRICS diplomacy, in which it can put forth an image of a softer nation to global audiences. For South African leaders, the BRICS forum and its diplomacy is a complement to its pursuit of South-South strategy. The country remains a significant regional economic and political player and joining the BRICS reflects the rising international influence and developing nature of global governance. The BRICS is thus the members' effort to address their common challenges in an international forum. The infectious personal chemistry of its leaders and their zeal to institutionalize critical issues that constitute the primary aspects of their leadership role remains the bloc's driving force. BRICS remains is the harbinger of a new financial architecture and it has the potential to benefit not just the member states of the organization, but the global financial system too.

BRICS and negotiating fair global governance in a "post-American world order"

Although originally an ideational construct, BRICS has become an economic construct of emerging powers for the negotiation of a "post-American world order." It has become a forum to articulate the voice of the emerging nations. This rationale has become the basis of convergence among the members. The BRICS was meant to be a purely economic category, but it now has to embrace some political and global governance concerns as well. It is now a force in discussing how the world should be governed and how countries should relate among themselves. Although there were divergent rationales among the member states concerning the alliance, but there remained certain commonalities among them. This includes a need to challenge the embedded power structure constituted by the West and to provide alternatives. The BRICS members individually and as a coalition faces challenges in the prevalent system of global governance dominated by the developed nations of the West. The nations constituting the bloc were capable of challenging this dominance as a group, a task that they were unable to do on an individual basis. Thus, BRICS as a regional grouping formed to bring forth a more inclusive governance architecture. The cooperation that exists among the five members of the group not only helps in fulfilling their interests as developing nations but also the global governance as a whole. It can be termed as an accelerator in the process of its alteration of the economic governance structure of the world too.

From the UN's perspective, global governance serves three purposes. Firstly, the management of trans-border relations among states. Secondly, to ensure a stable world order. And, thirdly to bring states together on issues of common concern that needs to be tackled. Thus, the primary variable that should guide the process of global governance is the creation of an equitable order. This can be ensured through the process of ensuring the equal participation of all the actors whose interest is concerned, and the upkeep of this factor is very well ensured by the BRICS.

Although currently, the worth of the BRICS members' economy is less than 15% of the G6 (US, UK, Japan, France, Germany, and Italy), the group still has the potential to emerge as a competitor to the Western developed states in their collective strength. The BRICS grouping can shape the contours of the world economy as together this regional organization accounts for about 43% of the total population of the world, 17% of the world trade, and about 30% of the GDP of the world. The global governance framework that BRICS seeks to develop will thus be vital for the development of the political stability of the world order in general and BRICS in particular.

The BRICS bloc seeks to influence global governance through several avenues to provide for a multilateral world order that is open and equitable. One priority area of influencing is through its economies; the prime reason for its birth as a bloc. The 2008 crisis led to the creation of a financial crisis in the international financial order and this then led to the pairing of the group of countries that were in a state of relative stability. This cooperation among them as a bloc increased their bargaining power, although for a temporary period. However, it has its benefits in the form of attaining the status of agenda setters at that period. This incident led to reforms in the IMF as was seen in the period of 2010 in the context of IMF quota reform. Thus, it shows the relevance of the grouping to create an alternative institution in the area of global governance. Similarly, the creation of the CRF and the NDB as agreed to in the Fifth annual Summit held in Durban can be regarded as another development that has the potential to undermine the Bretton Woods institution's dominance. However, it is important to note that to be on the upfront as a bloc to challenge the West in the aspect of global governance, BRICS has to maintain its economic growth and development.

CHAPTER FOUR: DESIGNING A VIABLE PATHWAY TO DE-DOLLARIZATION

Despite the challenges associated with the reserve currency status of the U.S. dollar, it remains the most dominant reserve currency and it will take significant strategic effort from the BRICS coalition to create a currency that can effectively compete with the U.S. dollar. There are tangible costs associated with being completely isolated from the dollar-based system. Typically, it is risky for young power coalition like the BRICS to voluntarily initiate a frontal revolution against an existing, entrenched, system. The de-dollarization initiatives of the BRICS nations will certainly attract resistance and reprisal actions from the U.S., including efforts to correct the "destabilizing asymmetry" of the dollar's exorbitant privilege. Efforts to displace the U.S. dollar dominance have to be well coordinated to grant the BRICS currency proper landing and mitigate the risk of being subject to the US dollar's hegemonic power, achieve higher autonomy, and have a broader influence in the global system.

The BRICS de-dollarization coalition emerged because its members and others are dissatisfied with the international status quo, including the dollar's exorbitant privilege, the incumbent US global leadership, and the existing rules and norms. As a rising power coalition, the BRICS need to continuously renegotiate and carve niches for itself in the international status quo as they seek to increase their influence and status, and aspire to become rule-makers and agenda-setters in the global financial system. Already, their dissatisfaction with the U.S. dollar dominance is commonly understood and is attracting more countries to join its counter-hegemonic coalition, especially those facing direct threats to their financial and geopolitical autonomy. The threats include being directly targeted by hostile and coercive policies or having the existing system experience a severe crisis or shock. Cutting Russia off the use of SWIFT is an example of a measure to coerce a targeted actor to change its behavior. This explains why Russia and China are at the forefront of the de-dollarization campaign, and why it has become easy for several other countries to desire to join the counter-hegemon coalition. As a coalition, it is expected that the BRICS bloc help its members survive the crisis and steer the system towards their preferred outcomes. Ultimately, for the de-dollarization coalition to materialize, the BRICS coalition must have appropriate entry points to influence the dollar system.

There are various entry points that the BRICS bloc can create or nurture to help it and its members mitigate the risk of operating in the dollar-based system. The possible pathways can be grouped into two. The first is to hedge the risk by developing an alternative nondollar-based system that allows the bloc to maintain direct economic and financial connections with other countries in the world without resorting to the dollar-based system. This is the so-called "go-it-alone" strategy. In this case, the BRICS bloc will create alternative institutions and mechanisms for doing business without using the U.S. dollar and various U.S.-linked financing and facilitation institutions. In other words, the BRICS countries will stay outside the existing dollar-based system and build new, nondollar structures.

The alternative approach is to pursue risk insurance and risk diversification by negotiating favorable deals using "voice" to initiate changes and improve the existing dollar-based system. This is the "reform the status quo" strategy, referring to the pursuit of reforms within the existing system to dilute the dollar's dominant currency status.

These two approaches are not mutually exclusive. The "go-it-alone" strategy can be used to create an "exit" pathway from the existing system. But it is often not possible to have a clean break away from an old deeply entrenched order. The BRICS countries can't readily have a system that is fully developed from the beginning. Hence, the need to negotiate passages for the coalition's strategy to grow with the existing system and even at maturity exist side-by-side with it. The new strategy can't be completely separated from the existing system because it still depends on it to mobilize the necessary resources to challenge the system.

The fact that the BRICS bloc has a strong go-it-alone (exit strategy) strengthens its bargaining power during the negotiations with the incumbent authorities. The threat of a possible exit can prompt the incumbent to see why the system should be reformed and support it. In other words, the threats of exit demonstrated by creating parallel institutions will serve as mild pressure to move the incumbent to accept and negotiate with the new entrant coalition. In their pursuit of autonomy and influence, the BRICS bloc will need both institutional and market mechanisms to implement its strategies.

The key propositions in the international relations literature to explain how a rising power can engage the incumbent are summarized in the following explanations

Develop alternative institutions and markets and support far-reaching system reforms

A rising power (or disruptor-innovator) seeking greater financial/geopolitical autonomy either in response to or to be shielded from a perceived threat of sanctions and currency risk, may decide to engage in developing or accelerating "go-it-alone" strategies involving the creation of alternative nondollar-based institutional and market mechanisms. It could do so alongside a fairly low-cost or near-term set of negotiations aiming to prompt reform of the status quo to help create entry points to ensure or enhance the accommodation of the disruptor's new institutions. In case, the BRICS countries can individually and as a group lobby other countries to understand and accept in principle the case for having new financial institutions like the NDB to pool resources for doing some of the things that the present World Bank, IMF, and development finance institutions are not doing. The BRICS can as well promote a global campaign including sponsoring studies to support the case for regional groups to exchange their currencies in cross-border trade as a prelude to the launch of its coalition currency. Promoting the use of national currencies in cross-border trade will progressively weaken the dollar's global influence and set the stage for introducing the coalition's currency. It is also possible to promote the emergence or expansion of nondollar-based equity markets in the existing global financial system to divert capital away from the dollar-based markets. Negotiating for the reform of the existing financial system to accommodate more cross-border trade with local currencies and the creation of regional currencies and growth of the non-dollar equity markets within the existing dollar-dominated system will grow non-dollar transactions. Pursuing this measure alongside activities of the NDB, CRA and the new BRIC-based SWIFT alternative may not necessarily cause the dollar to be replaced, but will allow the coalition's currency and possibly a few other regional currencies to emerge as dollar alternatives of different levels of importance.

The approach can be considered most valuable where, as obtained in this instance, the incumbent is well entrenched and the disruptor coalition has challenges with consensus building because some of the members share common interests with countries outside the disruptor coalition.

Using a go-it-alone strategy alone

The disruptor coalition may decide to go all out to focus on building its alternative markets and institutions. This applies more effectively where the membership of the disruptor coalition is huge and the average income per capita high enough for the population to buy. it is much easier to achieve these when the members sell more complementary than competitive products, making it possible for profitable cross-trading to exist among the member countries. For this to happen, it means that the BRICS membership must be extended to more countries with diverse potentials/resources and needs. This strategy applies better when the disruptor coalition members are under severe sanctions or immediate threat of sanctions and will have their international relationship stifled should they continue to depend on the U.S. dollar.

Using Negotiations Alone

In this case, the coalition members are not under pressure to exit the dollar system immediately and thus prioritizes the "reform the status quo" strategies in the near term. The group continues to remain in the existing system while promoting changes that support the growth of other reserve currencies and payment systems. Generally, ambitious rising powers seeking to diversify the system urgently will use both "reform the status quo" and "go-it-alone" de-dollarization strategies to increase their financial and geopolitical influence.

Expressions of the U.S. Dollar Dominant Currency Status

The U.S. dollar's dominant currency status can be divided into three primary areas, namely; the real economy, funding, and the dollar-investments. These three overarching categories cover the specific areas that constitute the structural constraint that any reactive de-dollarization initiative has to consider.

i. The U.S. dollar is the dominant global reserve currency and enjoys the highest weight in the Special Drawing Rights (SDR) basket. It is also the dominant invoicing currency in international trade; the leading currency across global financial infrastructure; and, it has the dominant pricing power in major global commodities.

ii. The dollar dominates the space of development financing, bank deposits, and global corporate borrowing.

iii. The dollar securities has proven to be the leading investible to run to in time of instability. Hence it dominates global equity markets and is the primary safe-haven currency in times of economic and financial crises.

The BRICS Strategic Attack on the U.S. Dollar

The BRICS coalition seeks greater financial and geopolitical influence, and is challenging the dominance of the US dollar by deploying de-dollarization pathways that address the strategic areas of the U.S. dollar dominance, namely; the real economy, funding, and investments. The BRICS coalition is so far the most comprehensive and effective challenge to the dollar hegemony since 1944 when the Bretton Woods conference made it the world's major reserve currency. The BRICS is using a combination of "go-it-alone" and "reform-the-status-quo" approaches, but the weight appears to be more on the side of "go-it-alone" than "reform-the-status-quo". The BRICS de-dollarization initiative is challenging the major specific areas in which the U.S. enjoys dominance, namely; production (real economy), currency exchange/payment system, and investment in dollar financial instruments. The BRICS coalition seeks to create an active and widely spread non-dollar club with new (alternative) institutions and markets that it controls as leverage. The product (or value addition) that it seeks to create is its alternative nondollar club good - alternative global financial institutions and markets. Although overcoming U.S. sanctions is the primary interest of the BRICS countries, the nondollar club is presented through broad engagement and popularized as a global public good.

Treating the nondollar club or de-dollarization initiative of the BRICS bloc as a global public good is understandable because it will not just help its members bypass coercive actions administered via the weaponized dollar, it will save the world from inflationary risks arising from the rising dollar value. Moreover, as the primary creator of the nondollar club, the BRICS countries are likely to become power brokers in the emerging new world order, and thus enjoy a higher status in the global political economic space than their followers.

The BRICS De-dollarization Initiative

The BRICS de-dollarization initiatives comprise the use of both institutional and market mechanisms to mitigate BRICS members' risk exposure to the dollar's hegemonic power. Currently, these initiatives include:

i. The NDB and development finance de-dollarization;

ii. Global oil trade de-dollarization;

iii. Global financial infrastructure de-dollarization through BRICS alternatives to SWIFT;

iv. BRICS promotion of de-dollarization initiatives by engaging with non-BRICS members;

v. Self-defense measures in US-led institutions against the dollar's dominance;

vi. Reforms of the global reserve currency structure;

vii. Efforts to diffuse the dollar's dominance as the vehicle currency in trade;

viii. BRICS' activities in global equity markets.

CHAPTER FIVE: COLLECTIVE MOBILIZATION FOR DE-DOLLARIZATION

The strength of the BRICS coalition is measured by the number of participants in its de-dollarization initiative. Successful cross-border settlements in international trade and finance require counterparties. Moreover, the formation of a nondollar global financial system requires the broad participation of state- and non-state actors. A higher number of both sets of participants implies the robustness of the de-dollarization initiative. Unilateral initiatives are to add up to the coalitional level, but they represent a low level of coalitional strength. The coalitional strength increases as more members of the BRICS act in unison. Once the coalition builds full consensus, it demonstrates greater coalitional strength. When the rising power coalition expands its de-dollarization initiatives beyond the group members and mobilizes a broader coalition, the coalitional strength is the highest.

BRICS as a Financial Coalition

The first BRIC summit in 2009 concluded with a clear statement from its leaders expressing their commitment to advancing the reform of international financial institutions, to reflect changes in the global economy. The members believe there is a strong need for a stable, predictable, and more diversified international monetary system. Since then, financial cooperation has been a consistent theme during every annual BRICS summit leading to several joint summit declarations. Several key milestones energize BRICS' commitment to diversifying the existing system. For example, between 2012 and 2017, BRICS established the NDB, collectively pushed for the use of local currency in development finance, and launched the CRA. In 2020, BRICS identified empowering local currencies as its long-term agenda item, thereby cementing its importance for the group in the future.

The first milestone is the establishment of the NDB and the CRA, which were initially proposed in 2012 and 2013 respectively, though both materialized in 2014. These two institutions resulted from the BRICS members' frustration with their limited progress in reforming the Bretton Woods institutions. BRICS created the NDB and CRA to mirror the functions of the World Bank and the IMF respectively, but operated under BRICS ownership and control. The NDB and CRA were both designed to help BRICS reduce their dependence on US dollar financing and the IMF. For example, it is stated in the founding documents of the NDB that the organization, "may provide financing in the local currency of the country in which the operation takes place". This statement positions the NDB as a development finance intermediary that uses local currencies to mobilize capital in international markets and provides financing for its members. This local currency financing function makes the NDB a "mini–World Bank." And in some sense, a better World Bank because it allows countries to use their currencies and offers loans to members with lesser strings attached. Offering loans to a country in its national currency allow it not to increase external US dollar debt.

The CRA is described by President Putin as BRICS IMF because it creates the foundation for the effective protection of the national economies of the member countries from crises in financial markets. It makes the pooled dollar reserves of USD100 billion available to provide liquidity support for members in times of minimal balance of payment (BoP) crisis. But the CRA is not intended as a lender of last resort. Rather, it provides the members with the first line of defense before they have to seek conditional help from the IMF. In that sense, the CRA is a go-it-alone strategy that aims to improve upon the status quo.

The Pandemic Induced De-Dollarization Commitments

The most recent de-dollarization milestone was achieved amid the COVID-19 pandemic at the Summit when the BRICS coalition agreed to reinforce and advance the current de-dollarization processes. Under Russia's chairmanship in 2020, the group jointly issued the Strategy for BRICS Economic Partnership 2025. This Strategy reiterated the members' long-standing commitment to reforming the Bretton Woods institutions. More importantly, it identifies several "priority areas of partnership" directly related to de-dollarization, including the following:

- To promote the use of local currencies in mutual payments;

- To strengthen BRICS cooperation on payments systems;

- To collaborate on the development of new financial technologies;

- To advance the CRA mechanism, continue cooperation on establishing the BRICS Local Currency Bond Fund, and facilitate development financing while expanding the use of local currencies.

Over the past two decades, BRICS has shown consistent commitment to reforming the global financial system and diversifying the global currency structure. Catalyzed by the global financial crisis and the COVID-19 pandemic, the group has implemented targeted policies and broadened areas of cooperation to help members reduce their dependence on the US dollar. The recent military conflict between India and China did not prevent the coalition members from deepening their economic partnership. This suggests a strong political will to pursue the BRICS de-dollarization agenda despite their divergence in other areas.

The Gradual Rise of BRICS Members' Currencies

As the de-dollarization programs of the BRICS countries are being implemented, the national currencies of member countries have progressively gained more market share in the dollar-dominated global economy. In the absence of a BRICS currency, the most direct way for BRICS to reduce their dependence on the US dollar is to increase the use of their national currencies in cross-border transactions. According to the latest Bank for International Settlements Triennial Survey (2019), the Chinese yuan was the 8th most actively traded currency, ranking just after the Swiss franc. This is a significant increase from its ranking of 35th in 2001. Additionally, the yuan is now the most actively traded emerging market currency. It reached 4.3% of total global turnover in 2019, a significant rise compared with 0.1% in 2004. The Indian rupee was the second most traded BRICS currency, in 16th position worldwide and accounting for 1.7% of global trade. The Russian ruble, Brazilian real, and South African rand were in the 17th, 20th, and 33rd positions, respectively.

Comparing the currency ranking position changes from 2004 to 2019, the increase in the Chinese yuan's active trading turnover was the largest. The growth in trading turnover for other BRICS currencies was not as rapid but steady. In contrast, the shares of leading global currencies, especially the euro, Japanese yen, and the British pound sterling have generally decreased, although they were still three of the top four most actively traded currencies.

Despite efforts to displace the U.S. dollar, it still maintains relative dominance in the currency market. But the collective market share of BRICS currencies, especially the yuan has slowly increased, albeit still far smaller than the US dollar's market share. The small increase in the market share of BRICS currencies did not cause the US dollar's market share to decrease. As the BRICS countries intensify the implementation of their currency internationalization policies, trading activities of BRICS currencies will slowly increase. But the increase may not necessarily come at the expense of the US dollar; rather, it may erode the market share of other major currencies, as data from 2004 to 2019 demonstrates. Thus, so far, the slight increase in the traded BRICS currencies can't be considered a credible challenge to the dollar's dominance in international settlements in any meaningful way. BRICS' insignificant currency share in global markets at present is disproportionate to their combined weight of approximately 16% of global trade

The BRICS Case for Reserve Currency Diversification

China's advocacy for reforming the dollar-based global financial system can be traced back to the 1997 Asian financial crisis. In the aftermath of this crisis, Dai Xianglong, then Governor of the People's Bank of China (PBoC), stated that the current international monetary and financial system can't continue to satisfy the needs of current global economic and financial development. Hence, the urgent need for reforms to check the instability associated with the role of international reserve currency played by a few countries' national currencies in the international monetary system. In particular, the current international financial system can't solve the balance of payments imbalance that has repeatedly caused spasms of international financial crises. Following the 2007–2008 global financial crisis, the Chinese Central Bank Governor, Zhou Xiaochuan, discussed the necessity of reforming the international monetary system and called for the creation of a global reserve currency that isn't a national currency of a country to avoid the prevailing system's deficiencies caused by using credit-based national currencies. Zhou's view is representative of the thoughts of leading Chinese officials who believe the era of a US dollar-dominated world is coming to an end. Although de-dollarization or making the yuan a reserve currency has not been made an official policy priority of the Chinese Government, Chinese academics and policy commentators have frequently criticized dollar hegemony and proposed various means to challenge it. Such critical discussions and commentaries have recently proliferated due to the deterioration of US-China relations, and growing threats of US sanctions against China in strategic areas such as advanced IT technology. Strategic rivalry with the

U.S. provides incentives for China to self-insure against risks in the US-led global system, not just for economic reasons but also for geopolitical and strategic reasons.

Even without the BRICS de-dollarization policy, China has been adjusting its strategies for renminbi internationalization through the development of offshore renminbi markets and bilateral currency swaps in the context of the Belt and Road Initiative. Chinese state-owned commercial banks are also more potent and more globalized compared to banking institutions in other BRICS members. China's policy banks, especially the China Development Bank and Exim Bank of China, now provide as much development financing as the World Bank does.

Russia's case for de-dollarization is primarily motivated by its geopolitical rivalry with the U.S. In 2012, Sergei

Ryabkov, Russia's Deputy Foreign Minister at the time, expressed concerns over the US dollar's role as the settlement unit of international trade and banking transactions and affirmed that it was necessary to be less dependent on the dollar. Also, President Putin expressed in an article that the BRICS members "are ready to work together with our partners to promote international financial regulation reforms and to overcome the excessive domination of the limited number of reserve currencies." Thereafter, Ryabkov disclosed that it is a "vital need" for Russia to "intensify work related to import substitution, reduction of dependence on US payment systems, on the dollar as a settling currency".

In his Speech at the Russian Parliament during his Inauguration for the fourth presidential term in May 2018, he expressed a strong commitment to further de-dollarize the Russian economy and defend Russia's economic sovereignty against US sanctions. He called for "getting free of the dollar burden" in the global oil trade and the Russian economy because the monopoly of the US dollar was "unreliable" and "dangerous" for global trade and the economies of many countries in the world. In August 2018, discussions on the need to de-dollarize the Russian economy intensified after the US Congress introduced a new bill that targeted Russian financial institutions. By October 2018, Putin endorsed a tentative de-dollarization plan to limit Russia's exposure to future US sanctions by reducing the use of the US dollar in international settlements and conducting international business using alternative currencies.

Brazil shares the Russian and Chinese enthusiasm for making BRICS a de-dollarization coalition. Former Brazilian President Lula da Silva argues that the BRICS has to attack the U.S. dollar's dominance directly by creating a currency that is independent of the US dollar. Three primary reasons may have incentivized Brazil to follow Russia and China's de-dollarization initiatives. First, Brazil's severe economic crisis since 2014 following the end of the commodity boom has fragmented the country's politics and led to the rise of the right-wing Bolsonaro administration. Under President Bolsonaro, the Brazilian government has sent mixed signals regarding its BRICS policy and has moved closer to Western powers. Second, Brazil has become more reliant on commodities exports, making the country more exposed to volatility in global markets and currency risks. According to UNCTADstat, Brazil's commodity exports represented 56.5% of total exports in 2008–2009. This number increased to 66.6% in the past ten years. Third, China has been Brazil's most important trading partner, and the economic and financial ties between the two countries have increasingly become closer.

The use of local currencies in bilateral settlements is beneficial for both Brazil and China. Brazil's close economic and financial ties with China and the real risks to the Brazilian economy due to its dependence on the US dollar suggest that Brazil is unlikely to openly champion BRICS de-dollarization initiatives. However, it is open to playing along and following them.

India was reluctant to join a BRICS de-dollarization coalition from the very beginning despite its support for other key issues on the BRICS agenda, such as reforming the IMF and World Bank. When Russia and China proposed to create a new global super-sovereign reserve currency to replace the US dollar in 2009, India distanced itself from such a challenge to the US dollar's supremacy but instead preferred a more modest approach of increasing the

IMF's SDR. The Indian government considered this Sino-Russian proposal more ideological than substantive and did not want to challenge the U.S. dollar and upset the U.S. especially at a time it was pressuring Pakistan on counterterrorism. While the U.S. treats Russia and China as strategic competitors, it considers India an important ally in the Indo-Pacific region and an important strategic partner. India's rivalry with China and the recent military standoff between the two countries have further prevented India from supporting China's attempt to replace the US dollar. In the context of BRICS, this means India will not support an explicit BRICS mobilization to dethrone the US dollar.

This by no means suggests that India is satisfied with the US dollar's dominance and would not seek to reduce its dependence on the US dollar. On the contrary, India not only has a strong interest in promoting the use of local currency in trade but also has taken initiatives to explore how to accomplish this. In 2012, India's Ministry of Commerce and Industry convened a Task Force to examine the use of the rupee in India's bilateral trade. The Task Force Report favored the idea of extending rupee trade to some oil-exporting countries. The Indian government formed a multi-agency task force with representatives from India's economic policymaking agencies to draw up a list of countries with which India could trade in rupees. India has also taken the lead in promoting BRICS financial cooperation and building BRICS financial institutions. For example, it was at the behest of the Indian finance minister that the BRICS in 2012 commissioned a joint working group to study the viability of setting up a BRICS Development Bank, which led to the creation of the NDB that promotes the use of local currencies in development finance. India has also promoted greater use of the rupee in international transactions in light of aggressive steps by China to internationalize the renminbi and US sanctions on Russia and Iran in 2018, which disrupted India's oil payments in US dollars.

The increase in currency exchange volatilities – especially growing volatilities in the US dollar – provides another incentive for India to de-dollarize its trade settlement, as India is among the most dollarized countries in trade invoicing. To give some context, 86% of India's imports relied on US dollar invoicing despite only 5% of India's imports originating in the U.S. Similarly, 86% of India's exports were invoiced in US dollars, while only 15% of India's exports were to the U.S. Therefore, although India is unlikely to play an explicit role in a BRICS coalition aiming to dethrone the US dollar, it will implicitly help reduce dollar dependence by supporting initiatives that promote the use of local currencies in trade and development finance.

South Africa saw US sanctions imposed against it in 1986 mostly lifted by 1991, and with the dismantling of apartheid, the relationship between the two countries has improved. The strength of this relationship partly explains South Africa's lack of a strong de-dollarization agenda. There are few public statements of South African leaders promoting the idea of BRICS as a de-dollarization coalition. But South Africa is tacitly behind the Russian and Chinese de-dollarization efforts. South African policymakers are aware of the risks associated with the US dollar's exorbitant privilege and like other BRICS coalition members are in support of the BRICS' initiatives to promote the use of local currencies in trade. For instance, following the 2011 BRICS Summit, South African Trade and Industry Minister Rob Davies said that BRICS members could protect themselves from exchange volatilities and benefit considerably by trading directly in their currencies and cutting out unstable internationally convertible currencies – specifically, the US dollar. During the 2013 BRICS Summit, Davies reiterated South Africa's interest in working out a mechanism within BRICS to settle trade in local currencies and emphasized that currency market volatility in developing countries "takes place not really because of any dynamics in our own country but because of dynamics in the world economy, and these dynamics are largely fueled by the U.S. abuse of its exorbitant privilege. Davies' comments expressed not only South Africa's frustration over its lack of autonomy in achieving economic security in global markets but also a shared frustration among developing countries within and beyond the BRICS group. South Africa has also accepted the broader use of the Chinese renminbi and has included the renminbi in its foreign exchange reserves to diversify currency risk. SWIFT data shows that between 2013 and 2015, the number of South Africa's renminbi payments increased by 191%, and by June 2015, the value of direct payments in renminbi between South Africa and China/Hong Kong reached 31.3%.

Thus generally, the BRICS bloc has demonstrated a consistent commitment to reforming the US dollar-based global financial system, as evidenced by the group's deepening cooperation on de-dollarization. Although not all BRICS members want to explicitly challenge the US dollar, there is a shared interest in reducing their dependence on it. All BRICS members have taken concrete steps towards de-dollarization to achieve greater autonomy. BRICS has also implemented targeted policies to help members reduce their dependence on the US dollar through the promotion of local currencies in trade and investment, both at the BRICS level and the sub-BRICS level.

Russia and China remain key leaders of the BRICS attempt to steer the group toward a de-dollarization coalition. Their primary motivation for de-dollarization includes rising geopolitical rivalries with the U.S. States and the growing risk of US sanctions. But Russia and China have taken different approaches to de-dollarization. Russia has been far more aggressive in its attempts to protect its economy from US sanctions and has been the most enthusiastic advocate of de-dollarization within BRICS. In contrast, China has made less noise but has been more capable of making substantive changes. China has not openly talked about de-dollarization, but it has emphasized its desire to "diversify" the system. The diversification of the system is a positive framing that focuses on China's prioritization of the system's stability and equality rather than the potentially counter-hegemonic nature of such actions. China considers the BRICS bloc as one of several platforms it can use to play its 'major country' diplomacy.

Brazil, India, and South Africa have all supported BRICS joint statements on reforming the existing dollar-centered global financial system over the past two decades. Each have also sought opportunities to promote the use of local currencies in international trade and development financing. Their consensus and practices concerning de-dollarization suggest that de-dollarization does not only take place in countries that are in geopolitical competition with the U.S. or under US sanctions. Rather, de-dollarization is important for developing countries that are price takers in global markets and lack autonomy in controlling their economic security. Therefore, it is a real priority for these countries to diversify and reduce their risk exposure to exogenous shocks and exchange volatilities due to the US dollar's dominance. This creates a baseline of shared interests among all countries that are subject to the U.S. dollar's privilege, whether they are U.S. allies or adversaries.

CHAPTER SIX: THE BRICS INSTITUTIONS AND MARKET MECHANISMS

BRICS has created a set of group-level de-dollarization club goods with a relatively high level of effectiveness, such as: (1) establishing and using the NDB to promote the use of member states currencies for trade, investments, and lending; (2) developing a common BRICS payment system to facilitate settlement using local currencies and a BRICS digital currency; and (3) at the sub-BRICS level, members have launched nondollar national payment systems that could form the basis for a BRICS alternative to the U.S. dollar-dominated SWIFT. The option for central bank digital currencies to be created is also explored. China has already launched its digital renminbi and a new nondollar market instrument, yuan oil futures, to de-dollarize the global oil trade. Collectively, BRICS members have leveraged their overlapping membership in non-Western multilateral organizations (e.g., the SCO) to promote the use of local currencies in international trade and finance and create new outreach opportunities for broader de-dollarization.

The NDB and De-dollarizing Development of Finance

The NDB has already raised funds in local currencies as part of its goal to weaken the stronghold of the US dollar and euro. A local currency lending program is implemented to help member countries mitigate the borrowers' foreign exchange risk and support the development of local capital markets. The NDB equally prioritizes the "use of borrowing country legislation, regulations and oversight procedures" whenever possible, as it sees "using the national system as the best way to strengthen a country's capacity and achieve better long-term development results". Through these programs, the NDB helps the BRICS countries improve their financial autonomy and reduce their reliance on dollar financing.

With the NDB, the BRICS countries can borrow from international capital markets at a much lower rate given that the NDB can obtain a higher credit rating than most of the BRICS members. For instance, since its establishment in 2014, Brazil, Russia, and South Africa have experienced several rounds of credit downgrading. Their deteriorated credit ratings increase their borrowing costs in international capital markets. But the NDB can borrow on their behalf for onward re-lending to them. Hence, all five members are committed to securing a higher credit rating for the NDB, and they succeeded: the NDB received a credit rating of AA+ from S&P and Fitch, which is higher than any individual BRICS member. This rating allows several BRICS members to borrow from global capital markets at much cheaper rates through the higher-rated NDB than they could on their own. The NDB's high credit rating allows it to raise capital relatively cheaply from the bond markets and lend onward at interest rates lower than what could be obtained by some BRICS sovereign borrowers themselves. The NDB's Vice President highlighted the NDB's ability to borrow at a lower cost as "a significant advantage," as it enables the NDB to pass on that benefit in the form of competitive interest rates when it extends loans to its members.

The NDB also helps the BRICS members reduce their reliance on dollar financing by extending loans in local currency and prioritizing local regulations and procedures where appropriate. For instance, about a quarter of the NDB's cumulative total approved financial assistance (about USD 15 billion) was given in local currencies by the end of 2019. Ultimately, financing 50% of projects with local currencies across the member states is targeted. The NDB raises funds in both U.S. dollars and euros, and in the national currencies of the member countries as well to progressively raise dependence on local currencies to help move away from loans denominated in dollars.

The NDB's General Strategy 2017–2021 considered local currency financing as a key component of NDB's value proposition to mitigate risks faced by borrowers and support the deepening of capital markets of member countries. It will "rely on local currency lending to the extent feasible to avoid foreign exchange risks for borrowers" and will actively seek opportunities to offer local currency loans "both to reduce risks to borrowers as well as to promote local capital markets". Besides promoting local currency lending, the NDB has also approved loans in other currencies such as the euro and the Swiss franc in 2019 to diversify its source of funding away from the US dollar.

To reduce the burden of dollar-denominated loans, the NDB must tap into nondollar capital markets for alternative sources of financing. It is also crucial for the NDB to obtain a high-quality credit rating in nondollar markets to reduce its cost of funding. The NDB has been moving in the right direction. It has obtained an AAA rating in capital markets not only within BRICS such as China and Russia but also beyond BRICS such as in Japan.

Additionally, Fitch assigned the NDB's "Euro Medium-Term Notes Program" an AA+ rating. Obtaining a wider credit rating in different currency areas paves the way for the NDB to tap into capital markets in those currency areas, allowing for the diversification of its funding source. Thus, the mission is not just to de-dollarize, but also expand the reach of the BRICS penetration into as many financial markets as possible.

The NDB's AAA credit rating in China allowed it to quickly tap into the Chinese capital market and issue a renminbi bond. Since then, the NDB has become the most active official sector issuer of Panda bonds, renminbi-denominated bonds sold in China by foreign issuers. The NDB had issued six Panda bonds worth RMB18 billion as of March 2021, with the most recent Panda bond issuance taking place in March 2021 when it sold RMB5 billion (USD767 million) Panda bond. This was the NDB's first issuance of the

Sustainable Development Goals bond. The bond proceeds were to be used to finance China's RMB7 billion Emergency Program Loan to help mitigate the impact of COVID-19 on the Chinese economy.

The NDB also planned to raise local capital funding from other BRICS members' capital markets and has registered bond programs therein. It registered its debut bond program in South Africa in April 2019. The registered maximum size of the bond program was 10 billion rands and is governed by South African law. In November 2019, the NDB registered its debut ruble bond program in Russia with a maximum size of RUB100 billion. The program was listed on the Moscow Exchange and is covered by the laws of the Russian Federation. The NDB equally planned to tap into the Indian rupee-denominated masala (foreign-issued) bond market in the second half of 2017, but this was postponed due to a significant drop in market liquidity and demand for masala bonds. However, the NDB has remained interested in the Indian rupee offshore market as part of its capital raising.

The NDB also helps its members with local currency loans. By the end of 2019, cumulative approved local currency loans represented 27% of the NDB's total portfolio. This number is remarkable because it is higher than the local currency loan percentages of other major multilateral development banks. This higher percentage is likely because the NDB has been offering renminbi loans since the beginning of its operations. The NDB also approved its first rand-denominated loans amounting to USD 1.2 billion equivalent in 2019. By the end of 2019, about two-thirds of the NDB's cumulative approvals for projects located in China were denominated in renminbi, and about half of its lending to South African borrowers was made in rand. This shows that the NDB has made good on its pledge to extend loans in local currencies.

The Yuan Oil Futures and De-dollarizing Global Oil Trade

As a multilateral institution governed by its members, the NDB represents a BRICS' coalitional challenge to the US dollar's dominance. There are also important de-dollarization trends in the global oil market used to support de-dollarization by expanding BRICS energy cooperation. The US dollar's hegemonic position is significantly diminished as the exclusive funding vehicle and pricing currency of the global oil trade. However, the world's leading crude oil pricing benchmarks, namely the West Texas Intermediate (WTI) and Brent, are priced in US dollars. Scholars have argued that the battle royale for de-dollarization is to be decided in the global commodity market, especially the USD 1.7 trillion oil market. The use of nondollar currencies in global oil markets is a serious challenge to the Eurodollar system.

The BRICS group is certainly strong enough to mount that challenge: in terms of consumption power, and is a bigger oil-importing bloc than the entire European Union. China is the world's largest energy importer, while Russia is the world's largest energy exporter. Both are mobilizing within BRICS to promote "yuan oil futures," thereby challenging the US dollar's hegemonic position in the global oil market.

Following the 2018 BRICS Summit, China launched yuan oil futures, a renminbi-denominated oil futures contract, on the Shanghai International Energy Exchange. China's new oil futures are priced in renminbi, and the renminbi is also convertible into gold on the Shanghai Gold Exchange and Hong Kong Gold Exchange. This process has led to China, the world's largest oil importer, having an entirely domestic infrastructure for trading oil using gold, and China's oil suppliers can receive payment in renminbi and immediately convert it into gold. This shift marks the beginning of a nondollar financial instrument and nondollar price determination mechanism for a major global commodity. Albeit, the Shanghai-traded yuan oil futures still lag behind rivals such as the London-traded Brent oil futures and the New York-traded WTI oil futures in terms of volume, but they have already surpassed comparable offerings traded in Tokyo and Dubai by a significant amount. The renminbi oil futures' accelerated growth has received the attention of leading central bankers in advanced economies. For example,

Bank of England Governor Mark Carney (2019) observed that "the renminbi is now more common than sterling in oil future benchmarks, despite having no share in the market before 2018.

Escalation of the US-China Trade War

With the recent escalation of the US–China trade war, China has accelerated its promotion of a possible petroyuan, renminbi-denominated oil trading. In 2021, Chinese Foreign Minister Wang Yi went on a week-long tour of Saudi Arabia, Turkey, Iran, the UAE, Bahrain, and Oman to drum in China's intention to secure long-term energy deals with major Gulf energy producers to dictate oil pricing terms and fuel the rise of the petroyuan. With China's push for the use of renminbi in oil pricing and trading and the strong global demand for a nondollar-denominated oil trading mechanism, "the renminbi-denominated oil trading is likely to become more significant, partially displacing US dollar oil trading in one market after another". The prospect of a petroyuan would make it possible for countries under US sanctions, especially major oil exporters such as Iran and Russia, to access global markets via an alternative currency and nondollar payment systems, thereby weakening the effectiveness of US sanctions power.

China's primary motivation for promoting its yuan oil futures is to encourage the use of the renminbi in oil trading and risk hedging, especially in the settling of physical oil deliveries to reduce exchange risks. The Chinese government cannot singlehandedly launch the yuan oil futures and ensure fast growth in trading volume because commodities trading requires buyers and sellers. The fact that the yuan oil futures have been launched successfully and the trading volume has expanded indicates that there is great interest in the market to de-dollarize the global oil trade.

Russia also has a strong interest in de-dollarizing the global oil trade because major Russian energy companies have been under US sanctions since the first Ukraine crisis in 2014. Being the world's largest oil and natural gas exporter, Russia's economic security revolves around vital oil and gas revenues. Oil and gas accounted for 60% of Russia's export revenues and nearly 40% of government revenues in 2017. BRICS supported Russia after the U.S. imposed sanctions on Russian companies. In June 2017, BRICS foreign ministers condemned "unilateral military intervention or economic sanctions in violation of international law and universally recognized norms of international relations".

China's launch of the yuan oil futures provides a crucial alternative trading platform for Russian oil companies and Russian oil consumers.

The potential of the yuan oil futures to advance global oil trade de-dollarization goes even further when considering the linkage to gold. China has sweetened the yuan oil futures by providing trading infrastructure to facilitate swapping oil into gold, with the renminbi serving as an intermediary funding step. If BRICS had their pricing benchmark for gold – rather than being subject to London or New York's pricing – this infrastructure would potentially complete the goal of de-dollarizing the global oil trade, making it possible to trade oil using gold with minimum exposure to exchange risk. Sergey Shvetsov, the First Deputy Chairman of Russia's central bank confirmed in 2017 that BRICS countries were discussing the possibility of establishing a single gold trading system, both within BRICS and at the level of bilateral contracts. Shvetsov previously raised this theme at the bilateral level during his visit to China in 2016. Such developments signal a potential BRICS alliance in the global physical gold market, where BRICS countries have major stakes: China, Russia, South Africa, and Brazil are major gold producers, and China and India are also the world's two largest gold consumers. A BRICS single gold trading system would facilitate the creation of a new gold pricing benchmark based upon global physical gold trading rather than gold derivatives. Combined with the gold-backed trading of yuan oil futures, oil producers could swap oil for gold rather than for US Treasury securities, further de-dollarizing the global oil market. Apart from de-dollarization, a BRICS single gold trading system would also help to strengthen domestic currency stability because it would free BRICS members from being subject to foreign pricing.

CHAPTER SEVEN: BRICS GLOBAL FINANCIAL INFRASTRUCTURE

In another effort to reduce their dependence on the US dollar, BRICS members have been building their global payment infrastructures for international transactions that are independent of the US dollar and can serve as alternatives to SWIFT, which currently is the leading messaging network for financial transactions worldwide. This allows BRICS members, especially those who are subject to US sanctions, to create their own rules for international banking and settlement. Moreover, by extending alternative financial infrastructure to other countries and regions, BRICS can create greater buy-in for their system and increase their financial and political influence using the alternative system.

Some BRICS members have independently developed their cross-border payment mechanisms in recent years. Both Russia and China have launched their national alternatives to the SWIFT global banking network and introduced their systems to broader global markets. China's development of the renminbi cross-border payment system took place in the context of building the BRI's financial infrastructure and renminbi internationalization. The added benefit of promoting broader use of the renminbi was to reduce foreign exchange risk and US sanctions risk for both China and its trading partners that may be under US sanctions, such as Iran or Russia. For Russia, establishing an international ruble payment system was the government's direct response to the heightened Western sanctions since the Ukraine crisis in 2014. China and Russia recently established a direct payment settlement system with each other, intending to combine it with payment systems in other BRICS members and BRI countries in Eurasia. Russian officials also revealed that the other BRICS members would support the establishment of a common payment system at the BRICS level.

BRICS countries, except South Africa, have developed their independent national payment systems, wholesale payment networks paired with a retail bank card network. China and Russia have been leading the development of independent national payment systems, which are the building blocks for a larger BRICS-controlled global payment system. An independent retail bank card network is a set of payment rails that establish protocols and procedures for the execution of retail payments and the exchange of related information among banks for final settlement over wholesale payment networks. An obvious benefit of having an independent retail bank card network, rather than relying upon leading American card network providers such as Visa or Mastercard, is to avoid the fees charged by these service providers. However, more importantly, if a country does not have its payment rails and relies upon those of Visa or Mastercard – as pre-2014 Russia and pre-2002 China did, and as South Africa currently does – then those payment rails could be unilaterally withdrawn as a part of US sanctions. This withdrawal leaves domestic consumers without the ability to conduct basic retail transactions using bank cards. Connecting these national payment rails to an alternative cross-border payment system would allow the entire life cycle of payments to be carried out while entirely bypassing the US dollar-denominated global system.

China's SWIFT Alternative

Over the past decade, China has broadened the international coverage of the renminbi-based financial infrastructure featuring China's cross-border payment system and UnionPay bank card network. China launched the Cross-Border Interbank Payment System (CIPS) for onshore renminbi clearance and settlement services in 2015. The goal is to promote greater use of the renminbi and support renminbi internationalization. Within two years, CIPS' direct participants in terms of high-value payment reached 28, and its indirect participants reached 574, covering 85 countries and regions. By the end of 2020, the number of CIPS' direct participants reached a total of 43, and the number of indirect participants reached 1159; 867 of which were in Asia – including 522 Chinese mainland indirect participants – 147 in Europe,

26 in North America, 20 in Oceania, 17 in South America and 39 in Africa. More than 3,000 banks and other financial institutions have conducted actual business through CIPS. By the end of 2020, CIPS was processing RMB135.7 billion (USD19.4 billion) daily. The annual business volume reached RMB45.3 trillion in 2020, despite the global economic slowdown caused by the COVID-19 pandemic.

CIPS allows global banks to clear cross-border renminbi transactions onshore directly instead of through offshore renminbi clearing banks. This empowers CIPS to serve as an alternative messaging system to SWIFT and thus reduce the risk of exposing transaction information to the U.S. thereby mitigating the effect of US sanctions. However, CIPS has not yet departed from SWIFT. It currently uses SWIFT and its standards for cross-border financial messaging to connect with the global system. CIPS also adopted the ISO 2022 international payments messaging standard to make it interoperable with other payment systems as well as with correspondent banks around the world. The adoption of the existing cross-border messaging standards serves China's interest in making CIPS a critical piece of financial infrastructure to promote renminbi internationalization.

Nonetheless, the current close connections between CIPS and SWIFT do not negate the potential of the new infrastructure to break away from the existing US-dominated cross-border payment system because the adoption of the existing messaging standard fast-tracks the adoption of CIPS by global financial institutions. The more global participants there are in CIPS, the wider its direct communication with foreign financial institutions – and therefore, the larger its potential to operate independently. Moreover, the broader adoption of CIPS will also accelerate the wider use of the renminbi in the international financial system.

Although the renminbi has not yet become an international currency, like the US dollar, UnionPay – China's central bank-approved independent bank card network launched in 2002 – has achieved a significant global presence. It has grown to be the largest supplier of bank payment cards, with over 7.5 billion cards issued worldwide, more than Visa and Mastercard combined. UnionPay began to expand overseas in 2004 and quickly established a global payment network. By March 2021, the UnionPay acceptance network extended to 180 countries and regions, over half of which also accept UnionPay mobile payments and more than 150 million UnionPay cards have been issued in 67 countries and regions outside Mainland China. The globalization of UnionPay promotes the use of the renminbi in cross-border settlements via outbound

Chinese tourism consumption and international merchandise transactions.

UnionPay is widely accepted in all BRICS countries. In Brazil, UnionPay cards were first accepted at Brazilian ATMs in 2006. In March 2021, the acceptance rate of UnionPay bank cards reached 70%. In Russia, UnionPay partnered with the Russian National Payments Card System in 2016, allowing both payment networks to accept UnionPay cards and Russian bank cards. This agreement broadened the international use of Russian bank cards. UnionPay's acceptance rate in Russia reached over 90% in 2019. UnionPay has also promoted its mobile payment feature in Russia. In 2018, UnionPay and Huawei jointly launched their Huawei Pay service in Russia, which was their first joint international market launch. In 2020, UnionPay partnered with Russia's Solidarnost Bank and Huawei to accelerate contactless payments in Russia and enable cardholders to use Huawei Pay on their Huawei or Honor smartphones.

Regarding India, in 2018, the Reserve Bank of India approved the cooperation between UnionPay and the National Payments Corporation of India, which runs the country's "RuPay" bank card network. This approval allowed UnionPay cardholders to use all ATMs and point-of-sale terminals in India to withdraw cash or conduct transactions using the Indian rupee. In December 2018, UnionPay cards were accepted at over 90 percent of ATMs in India. South Africa's business with UnionPay started in 2008. Within a decade, UnionPay bank cards became widely accepted for withdrawal service by most ATMs of the four major South African banks. In 2019, the Standard Bank of South Africa launched its UnionPay cards in both virtual and physical form to local account holders to facilitate their payments in China.

Besides working with local banks, UnionPay has also been working with retailers of all sizes in South Africa to enable their point-of-sale (POS) terminals at checkout counters across the country. Overall, the growth of UnionPay in day-to-day transactions combined with the CIPS infrastructure gives China and other BRICS members an option to de-dollarize bilateral payments using the renminbi as an alternative.

Russia SWIFT Alternative

Russia's de-dollarization initiatives started in 2014 in the wake of US sanctions. Following Russia's annexation of Crimea, President Barack Obama signed Executive Order No. 13661, which targeted bank cards issued by seven Russian banks. Both Visa and Mastercard stopped processing transactions for their

Russian customers, and about 500,000 credit cards and debit cards issued by these seven Russian banks found their payment function frozen. This severely affected Russia's domestic and international economic exchanges. Moreover, the U.S. and the UK also threatened to cut off Russia from SWIFT. In this context, Russia began building two pieces of the financial infrastructure that are critical for reducing its exposure to US sanctions, namely: (1) an independent national payment system to serve as Russia's alternative to Visa or Mastercard; and (2) a proprietary financial messaging system as Russia's equivalent to SWIFT.

Russia's de-dollarization of financial infrastructure started when the Russian State Duma passed the National Payment Card System (NSPK) Act in 2014. This Act established the National Payment Card System Joint Stock Company as the main operation and settlement center of the NSPK, which was owned by Russia's central bank. In July 2015, through public tender in Russia, the card was named "MIR," which means both "world" and "peace" in Russian. By August 2017, more than 13.9 million MIR cards had been issued in Russia (representing 10% of the Russian population). By the first half of 2019, 312 banks in Russia had joined the system. Practically all trade and service points, including cafes, shops, restaurants, and petrol stations, now accept payments with MIR cards. MIR cards are also welcomed in sanctions-hit Crimea, where Western banks have been prohibited from operating. MIR's performance shows other governments how to challenge established payments giants based in the U.S. such as Visa and Mastercard.

Since 2014, Russia has also been developing its proprietary financial messaging system called "System for Transfer of Financial Messages"

(SPFS) as the Russian analog to SWIFT. It can be connected to both foreign banks and foreign legal entities. According to the director of the Bank of Russia's national payment system Alla Bakina, 8 foreign banks and 34 legal entities signed agreements to join the SPFS by 2019. Traffic through the system has been growing and accounted for around 15% of all internal traffic in 2019, up from 10 to 11% in 2018. Moreover, Russia has been actively seeking to expand SPFS's international presence. Opening up SPFS to foreign banks was part of President Putin's agenda to further undermine the US dollar after his election victory in 2018. In 2019, Russia and Iran connected their financial messaging systems, linking banks in both countries through SPFS and SEPAM (the Iranian alternative to SWIFT). Russia also introduced SPFS to banks in the Eurasian Economic Union (EEU) region. The same year,

Russian Finance Minister Anton Siluanov signed an agreement with Turkey to start using the ruble and the lira in cross-border payments and settlements, greatly increasing the possibility of connecting Turkish banks and companies to SPFS and using Russian MIR cards in Turkey. Besides the EEU region and Turkey, Russia also expressed interest in linking SPFS with other countries in the Middle East and European region.

"China-Russia Plus" Coalition to Create a SWIFT Alternative

Russia has sought to mobilize its BRICS partners, particularly China, to achieve wider acceptance of its MIR card system and greater international coverage of its SPFS infrastructure. In November 2016, Prime Minister Medvedev said that Russia desired a mutually compatible payments system with China that would harmonize the two countries' national payment systems to preemptively deal with the risk of being cut off from SWIFT. He also said that Russia and China discussed the launch of a new cross-border payment system for direct trade invoices settlements in the renminbi and ruble. Medvedev made it clear that this initiative was an attempt to move away from the current dollar-dominated financial system and bypass Western sanctions. In June 2019, Russia and China agreed to deepen cooperation in national payment card systems and cross-border payments in national currencies. In March 2021, Russian Foreign Minister Sergei Lavrov again called for China to work with Russia to reduce their dependence on the US dollar and Western payment systems and push back against the West's "ideological agenda".

On China's side, the PBoC has improved the efficiency of transactions between the two national currencies. In October 2017, the PBoC approved the China Foreign Exchange Trading System (CFETS) to institute a payment versus payment (PVP) system to facilitate financial transactions between the renminbi and ruble. This PVP system can shorten the delivery time lag between the two currencies from at least a day to only a few seconds, which is a major improvement in transaction efficiency and will greatly reduce foreign exchange transaction risk. This PVP system was the very first of its kind. Its launch marked the official establishment of a PVP mechanism for transactions between the renminbi and foreign currencies in China's foreign exchange market.

India was reported to have expressed interest in jointly exploring an alternative to SWIFT with Russia and China to conduct trade with countries under US sanctions. While India currently does not have its domestic financial messaging system, it has plans to link a service that is currently under development with Russia's SPFS, which could be linked with China's CIPS. Once this materialized, this linked system would cover most parts of the world.

CHAPTER EIGHT: A COMMON BRICS PAYMENT SYSTEM AND DIGITAL CURRENCY

An ambitious BRICS coalition de-dollarization initiative is the "BRICS Pay" system. It is a single contactless payment system that connects BRICS' national payment systems with an integrated cloud platform for payment. BRICS Pay will not duplicate the national payment systems that are already in place in the member countries; rather, the system leverages the latest fintech innovations in BRICS countries to integrate BRICS members' payment systems. BRICS Pay will link the credit or debit cards of BRICS citizens to online wallets, which will be accessible 24/7 for payment via a mobile application installed on smartphones. The BRICS Pay system is part of BRICS' collective effort to establish a common system for retail payments and transactions between its members. However, BRICS is willing to expand its scope, and non-BRICS countries will also be able to use the platform. The pilot project kicked off in South Africa in early April 2019. In 2020, the Russian BRICS Presidency proposed the idea of a commercial "BRICS Pay" for "BRICS Plus" countries for the consideration of the BRICS Business Council.

The BRICS Pay hopes to serve as an integrated is that this proposed integrated payment system that would make possible the use of BRICS members' national currencies as a direct basis of exchange for external payments. Currently, external settlements between BRICS members still require conversion into US dollars and in many cases the engagement of US banks. For example, a yuan-ruble non-cash settlement using UnionPay cannot happen directly; it must be converted into US dollars first. With BRICS Pay, conversion to the US dollar and US banks would no longer be necessary because payments would be settled using the national currencies of the BRICS members. The BRICS Pay system will also allow the members to reduce their dependence on international payment organizations such as SWIFT, Visa, and Mastercard. It could potentially give BRICS members a shared competitive advantage to compete with traditional banks in the global financial services market, currently dominated by US banks, as well as US rules and norms. The integrated BRICS Pay system connecting the national payment systems of BRICS members while also allowing non-BRICS countries to participate could potentially disrupt the financial dominance of the incumbent Western global financial powerhouses. Russia has expressed that the foundation of a new international payment system is a priority for BRICS as a group which is driven by "increasing non-market risks of the global payment infrastructure".

Using Blockchain Technology to Build a BRICS Digital Currency

Building a common framework for BRICS Pay is an effort toward de-dollarization through the conventional route of promoting local fiat currencies in cross-border settlements. Meanwhile, BRICS has also been exploring an unconventional route toward this end. One approach is the use of blockchain technology to build a BRICS digital currency. During the

BRICS Xiamen Summit in 2017, the BRICS Finance Committee discussed the possibility of replacing the US dollar with a BRICS cryptocurrency in settlements among members. At the 2018 BRICS Summit, BRICS countries' development banks signed an agreement to cooperate on blockchain research and digital economy development, thereby working on frontier technological development together. They agreed to form a joint research working group, set a research agenda, and carry out research toward identifying potential applications of blockchain technology in the financial sector, particularly in infrastructure financing. The 2019 BRICS Summit further prioritized the bloc's cooperation in blockchain and digital economy. The BRICS Business Council supported the idea of creating a single payment system for settlements between BRICS members during this summit. The head of the Russian Direct

Investment Fund, Kirill Dmitriev, noted that an efficiently operated BRICS payment system can facilitate settlements in national currencies and ensure the stability of settlements and investments among the BRICS countries, which form more than 20% of the global influx of foreign direct investment. A BRICS cryptocurrency could be integrated into the common BRICS payment framework, and it would take the form of a paperless document flow to facilitate transactions. Given that BRICS members have agreed upon blockchain R&D cooperation, they can develop this system using blockchain technology.

Also, BRICS members have been developing their own central bank digital currency (CBDC) that could potentially revolutionize the global currency system. China started its CBDC project in 2014 and revealed its strategic agenda in 2016. Since 2020,

China has launched the "Digital Currency Electronic Payment" program in several Chinese cities, including Shenzhen. In 2021, cross-border tests of digital renminbi were conducted in Hong Kong with the Hong Kong Monetary Authority. Since then, there have been discussions regarding the broadening and deepening of the use of digital renminbi. The rollout of digital renminbi payment infrastructure in Hong Kong could increase the speed of cross-border payment and clearing processes while also cutting costs. If successful, the digital renminbi may help bypass the global bank-based system and allow China to make direct payments to other countries, diminishing the impact of US sanctions. However, the Deputy Governor of the PBoC Li Bo maintains that China's digital renminbi is aimed at domestic use rather than to replace the US dollar.

Other BRICS members have explored their options for CBDC. The Central

Bank of Brazil already did some groundwork and laid the critical infrastructure for the issuance of a CBDC. In 2020, it launched its blockchain platform called PIER (Platform for Information Integration of Regulatory Entities), which allows for the exchange of data between financial regulatory authorities. It also launched a 24/7 instant payment system called "PIX" to improve the efficiency and competitiveness of the retail payment market in Brazil. It was reported that "PIX" supports peer-to-peer and business-to-business transactions in 10 seconds or less via mobile phone, internet banking, and select ATMs.

Russia has also fast-tracked its national digital currency development. Elvira Nabiullina, Governor of Russia's central bank, referred to digital currency as "the future for our financial system because it correlates with the development of the digital economy". In 2020, Russia's central bank outlined

Russia's plan for a digital ruble, aiming to launch a pilot program at the end of 2021. As of October 2020, at least five Russian banks had expressed interest in participating in future, non-public tests of the digital ruble.

South Africa has been interested in the prospect of its own CBDC. The South African Reserve Bank has been conducting research on CBDC since late 2016. It completed a 14-week proof-of-concept trial for "Project Khokha" (Khokha means 'pay' in the South African Zulu language), testing the idea of a commercial payment system for interbank settlement using a tokenized South African rand on Ethereum-based blockchain Quorum. The test results showed that "the typical daily volume of the South African payments system could be processed in less than two hours with full confidentiality of transactions and settlement finality". The central bank launched "Project Khokha 2" in

February 2021 to explore the use of both a wholesale CBDC and a wholesale privately issued settlement token for interbank settlement.

Following China's launch of the digital renminbi, the Indian government proposed to prohibit all private cryptocurrencies and create a framework for an official digital currency in February 2021. In 2018, the announced that it had constituted a team to study the desirability and feasibility of a CBDC. According to Governor Shaktikanta Das, the Reserve Bank of India has been preparing to launch its digital currency.

Currently, none of the alternative payment systems discussed above has achieved truly global status, except China's UnionPay network. However, the proliferation of these substitutes shows that BRICS members are eager to take defensive measures and build their versions of financial infrastructures to sanction-proof their international transactions.

BRICS Plus: De-dollarization Mobilization beyond BRICS

The BRICS countries have leveraged their overlapping memberships in other non-Western multilateral institutions to build wider coalitions around their "go-it-alone" de-dollarization initiatives. Annual BRICS summits have been a convenient platform for such mobilization. For example, EEU and SCO members and observers were invited to the 2015 BRICS Summit to gain their support for de-dollarization efforts. During the meeting, Chinese President Xi emphasized that the BRICS, the SCO, and the EEU are all influential mechanisms of cooperation and that the gathering of state leaders sent out a positive signal of unity and cooperation to emerging markets and other developing countries. In 2017, the BRICS leaders, together with the leaders of Egypt, Guinea, Tajikistan, Mexico, and Thailand, held the "Dialogue of Emerging Market and Developing Countries" on the margins of the BRICS Xiamen Summit. This dialogue marked the launch of the China-initiated "BRICS Plus." BRICS Plus expands the BRICS platform to bring in other countries and regional integration institutions, such as the Mercosur, the SCO, EEU, the South African Customs Union, South Asian Association for Regional Cooperation, and ASEAN + China. BRICS Plus brings together thirty-five countries to form an expanded platform that can coordinate policies with BRICS regional partners across the four continents. It thus provides a convenient venue for de-dollarization policy coordination and nondollar financial infrastructure construction.

A notable example of broader mobilization through the BRICS Plus informal institution is a sub-group of the BRICS Plus, namely, the SCO. Several BRICS members are members of the SCO. Both China and Russia are founding members, and India joined as a full member in 2017. With three of the five BRICS members being also SCO members, these two non-Western institutions will likely conduct policy sharing and policy coordination through both platforms, including policies designed to reduce their dependence on the US dollar. The SCO was initially established for security cooperation, but it has gradually taken on economic dimensions as well. Before the Shanghai Summit in 2006, Shanghai Cooperation Organization (SCO) members launched the "SCO Mechanism of Interbank Cooperation." During the Shanghai Summit, members also launched the SCO Business Council to facilitate greater economic cooperation within the SCO framework. BRICS has initiated similar efforts, launching the BRICS Interbank Cooperation Mechanism in 2010 and the BRICS Business Council in 2013. In 2020, the SCO announced plans to further enhance financial cooperation and expressed willingness to continue discussions on the establishment of the SCO Development Bank and the SCO Development Fund. The SCO members underscored the importance of a joint approach to the use of national currencies in mutual settlements between interested SCO member states. The development of SCO financial cooperation initiatives suggests that China, India, and Russia can potentially introduce de-dollarization policies in the SCO and achieve synergies with similar initiatives in BRICS policy platforms.

The SCO's consideration of launching its development bank suggests a BRICS-like path: building formal institutions that can promote the use of local currencies in BRICS' development finance and reduce risks associated with US dollar financing. The convergence in institutional arrangement and mandates between the SCO and BRICS set the foundation for closer economic and financial policy cooperation between them. Such similarities can provide formal channels for further policy coordination between these two developing-country coalitions on issues such as: expanding the scale and scope of bilateral currency swaps, promoting the use of local currencies in cross-border trade and investment, and eventually reducing the countries' dependence on the US dollar. A closer alignment between BRICS and SCO toward de-dollarization has already been taking place. SCO Secretary-General Vladimir Norov recently confirmed that the SCO members have been working on a gradual transition to mutual settlements in national currencies, with representatives of the SCO Interbank Consortium already engaged in this activity. He also raised the need for the SCO to establish partnerships with the AIIB, the NDB, and the Silk Road Fund to fully unlock the investment potential of the SCO. In 2020, SCO Finance Ministers agreed to send recommendations to finalize a roadmap to promote bilateral trade and investments and issue bonds using local currencies.

Summarily, BRICS and its members have pursued de-dollarization through the "go-it-alone" strategy using both institutional and market mechanisms to achieve greater autonomy and influence. The specific examples of the NDB and development finance de-dollarization, BRICS commitments to develop a BRICS alternative to SWIFT, and the members' joint vision for a BRICS digital currency suggest that BRICS has demonstrated a high level of coalitional strength in executing highly effective de-dollarization initiatives. These are club goods that could serve as critical elements for developing an alternative nondollar global financial system and help shield members from dollar volatility and US sanction risk. Also, powerful sub-coalitional dynamics are at play. De-dollarization initiatives at the sub-BRICS level have been most active, with Russia and China being the two pivotal states leading these "go-it-alone" initiatives. A Russia–China de-dollarization mini-coalition is emerging, with the potential for broader participation by other countries under US sanctions, such as Iran. Deteriorating US–China relations will very likely drive China to move closer to Russia and double down on de-dollarization in the future.

Additionally, BRICS has also attempted to create broader coalitions by leveraging the members' overlapping memberships in other non-

Western organizations, such as the use of BRICS Plus and its engagement with SCO and EEU. Although such broader mobilization has not yet yielded significant tangible results and has not led to any broader de-dollarization of public goods, BRICS has certainly demonstrated its leadership as the rule maker and agenda setter for promoting the use of local currencies in international trade and finance, compatible to achieve higher international influence.

The Russian and Chinese "go-it-alone" de-dollarization initiatives are the most dominant influence. But so far, the combination of country- and coalition-level actions are unlikely to achieve speedy de-dollarization as expected for three main reasons, as follows:

First, the limited capacity of the NDB to raise funds means BRICS cannot achieve full de-dollarization in international borrowing for development finance. All BRICS members have been strongly in favor of promoting local currency development financing through the NDB, but the NDB's capacity is much more limited relative to traditional development financiers such as the World Bank or the Asian Development Bank. While the NDB has been considering potential expansion, its size, and scope constrain BRICS collective de-dollarization potential.

Second, not all BRICS members have the resources or capacity to sponsor their market infrastructures or instruments. So far, China and Russia have more compelling reasons and the capacity to develop their alternatives to SWIFT and seek to connect them. More so, only China's market size is large and influential enough to launch an alternative oil futures contract, like the yuan oil futures, to the US dollar market. Thus, the BRICS members can't abandon the US dollar-based financial infrastructure that soon.

Third, the internal geopolitical dynamics within BRICS and its members' relationships with the U.S. may prevent BRICS from formally making the group a de-dollarization advocacy coalition, which would have been the fastest way to implement the "go-it-alone" strategy and gain followers.

CHAPTER NINE: NEGOTIATING FOR REFORMS OF THE EXISTING SYSTEM

The BRICS alliance is negotiating to reform the status quo alongside its "go-it-alone" initiatives. The "reform-the-status-quo" strategy aims to dilute the US dollar's dominance in the existing global financial system. The BRICS members seek to diversify their reserve assets at the individual state level and at the same time collectively build an internal layer of support through the dollar-based CRA to modify their dependence on the IMF and negotiate the reform of the IMF SDR. The BRICS stock exchanges have also formed an alliance that is reshaping global equity markets. Such BRICS-level initiatives demonstrate BRICS' strength as a de-dollarization coalition working within the existing dollar-based system to improve BRICS autonomy and influence. At the sub-BRICS level, members have been promoting the use of local currencies in bilateral trade and strengthening internal currency cooperation by using bilateral currency swaps to diffuse the US dollar's dominance as the vehicle currency for global business. These sub-BRICS initiatives do not directly improve the global influence of the members, but they help achieve the goal of greater autonomy by reducing exchange risk in bilateral trade and exposure to US sanctions.

A key dominance factor of the U.S. dollar is the common adoption of US Treasury securities as the proxy for risk-free assets in global financial markets. Many central banks and sovereign institutional investors, including the BRICS central banks and other sovereign fund investors. Having a concentrated portfolio of US Treasury securities has not only increased the opportunity costs for the BRICS members in times of a weakening US dollar, but it equally increases their geopolitical vulnerability to US sanctions. To strengthen their self-defense against the US dollar hegemony, major BRICS central banks, especially the Bank of Russia, have diversified their reserve assets by reducing their holdings of US Treasury securities. Moreover, BRICS also established CRA as a pooled US dollar reserve and an internal first line of defense to help members during the small-scale balance of payments shortfalls. All of these measures allow the BRICS members to strengthen their self-defense against volatilities in the US dollar and improve their internal support for liquidity in times of dollar shortages.

Russia has been the most aggressive among BRICS in substituting US dollar reserves with alternative reserve assets. Since 2013, the Bank of Russia has been reducing the number of transactions conducted in US dollars and has increased the use of euros, renminbi, and rubles in settlements. In April 2018, following a new round of stringent US sanctions on Russia, the Bank changed the structure of its reserve assets, reducing the dollar's share in favor of the yuan and the euro. It also expedited the withdrawal of its reserves out of US Treasury bonds. After the Biden administration imposed new sanctions on Russia for cyberattacks and election interference in April 2021, Russia accelerated the pace of de-dollarizing its reserve assets. Russia decided to completely remove dollar assets from its National Wealth Fund (NWF), whose portfolio forms part of Russia's currency and gold reserves and had a value of USD 186 billion by the end of May 2021.

The renminbi is a big beneficiary of the de-dollarization of Russian reserves. In early 2019, its central bank invested USD44 billion into the renminbi, increasing its share in Russia's foreign exchange reserves from 5% to 15%. Russia's renminbi holdings are about ten times the global average for central banks, accounting for about a quarter of global renminbi reserves. With NWF's ongoing de-dollarization, this number is likely to increase. In 2021, the Kremlin allowed Russia's sovereign wealth fund to invest in renminbi and Chinese state bonds. Russia's aggressive de-dollarization policies are conducive to strengthening a potential Russia–China partnership for de-dollarization. Russian experts have suggested that Russia's push to accumulate the renminbi is not just about diversifying reserves but also about encouraging China to become more assertive in challenging US global economic leadership.

Besides replacing US dollar reserves with other currencies, the Bank of Russia has also been implementing a gold strategy to move away from US assets. It has been the largest buyer of gold in the past few years, quadrupling Russia's gold reserves over the past decade: between 2018 and 2019, the value of Russia's gold reserves increased by 42%, to USD109.5 billion. As a result, gold has taken up the largest share of Russia's total reserves since 2000. By June 2020, gold constituted 23% of the reserves of Russia's central bank, while the share of US dollar assets declined to 22%. Russia's gold strategy has made it the leader among BRICS members measured by the percentage of gold in total reserves.

The BRICS CRA helps to further strengthen the BRICS collective defense against the balance of payments crises due to US dollar shortages. BRICS members are allowed to draw from the CRA's collective pool of USD100 billion reserves through swaps using their currencies in times of need. Some scholars view the CRA as an institution that challenges the IMF, especially in light of BRICS' dissatisfaction with the conditionalities of IMF lending and the domination of Western powers in the IMF. Yet the CRA remains dependent on the IMF, and it cannot serve as a substitute for the IMF. Only 30% of accessible CRA funds are available to BRICS members on demand, whereas accessing the remaining 70% requires arrangements with the IMF. This provisional dependence on the IMF preserves the sustainability of the CRA's pooled US dollar reserves. If the maximum amount is insufficient, then BRICS members would resort to the IMF. This establishes an internal first line of defense for BRICS members up to the authorized amount. Thus, the CRA modifies BRICS' dependence on IMF's rescuing mechanisms by adding a layer of defense and acts within and conditional upon the existing dollar-based system while strengthening BRICS' self-defense against a US dollar shortage.

Reforming the Global Reserve Currency Structure

The BRICS members have collectively attempted to disrupt the US dollar's dominant position in the current global reserve currency structure by promoting the reform of the IMF's SDR and supporting the renminbi's inclusion into the SDR basket. These initiatives are part of the BRICS' broader efforts to reform the existing multilateral international financial institutions.

China has long expressed its desire to have the global reserves currency structure changed and advocated for giving the SDR a greater role. In March 2009, the PBoC Governor, Zhou Xiaochuan, called for making the SDR into a "super-sovereign reserve currency"; a position that the UN supports. The UN proposal for establishing a new Global Reserve System based on the IMF's SDR notes that the global imbalances played an important role in the 2007-2008 financial crisis, and should be addressed by creating a new Global Reserve System founded upon an expanded SDR, with regular or cyclically adjusted emissions calibrated to the size of reserve accumulations. This will contribute to global stability, economic strength, and global equity. Russia was among the first countries to express its support for the UN proposal. Russia and China "have similar positions" on the reform of the international financial system.

In June 2009, days before the BRIC summit, President Dmitry Medvedev expressed Russia's dissatisfaction with the existing reserve currency structure and called upon the IMF to expand the SDR basket to include the renminbi, commodity currencies such as the ruble, and gold to create a supranational reserve currency for international settlements. Russia raised this issue again during the first BRIC summit and revealed its plan to reduce the share of US Treasury bills in its USD400 billion reserves. This sentiment resonated with China and Brazil's decision to invest USD40 billion and USD10 billion, respectively, in IMF bonds, with another USD10 billion from India. In this context, the issue of reforming the global reserve currency structure has become an important issue for BRICS, and members have shown their collective commitment to diversifying their reserves away from being overly concentrated in US dollar assets.

The 2011 BRICS Summit highlighted BRICS members' shared interests in reforming the existing reserve currency structure. BRICS leaders declared their support for the reform and improvement of the international monetary system, with a broad-based international reserve currency system that promotes stability and certainty. They welcome the proposal on expanding the SDR's role in the existing international monetary system including the composition of the SDR basket of currencies. This position was during the 2013 BRICS summit. BRICS members also jointly expressed their support for the inclusion of the renminbi into the SDR basket in October 2016 in their Goa Declaration.

BRICS' efforts to reform the existing system have thus far led to limited success. BRICS combined voting rights at the World Bank and IMF and BRICS total SDR quota is below 15% of the total. These numbers are still misaligned with BRICS' collective economic power, which represents close to a quarter of global GDP. This limited success indicates the mounting difficulty facing BRICS members to further advance their voice and representation in the existing global system. Reforming the system through negotiation from within is thus seriously challenged compared to the "go-it-alone" strategies.

Weakening the Dollar's Dominance as the Vehicle Currency in Trade

BRICS members are keen to promote the use of their national currencies in trade settlements, and they have discussed this issue at BRICS summits for nearly two decades. High-level agreements on trade de-dollarization, as expressed in BRICS joint statements, have materialized through bilateral agreements among the members. For example, in June 2009, China and Russia reached an agreement to move toward settling bilateral trade in local currencies. A few days later, China and Brazil also announced an "initial understanding" to gradually eliminate the US dollar in their bilateral trade, which was estimated to be USD 40 billion at that time. During the 2013 BRICS Summit, India's Commerce and Industry Minister, Anand Sharma, discussed his proposal to settle bilateral payments in local currencies with his South African counterpart Rob Davies. In 2015, South Africa's Investec Bank and the China Export-Import Bank acted on this proposal and signed a Strategic Cooperation Agreement, which included the use of the renminbi as a settlement currency in trade. In June 2016, the PBoC added the South African rand, allowing for direct trading on the Chinese interbank market.

To further promote the use of local currencies in bilateral trade, the BRICS members augmented their agreements through a series of bilateral currency swaps, especially between China and other BRICS members. In 2013, the new China-Brazil bilateral swap agreement allowed them to trade in local currencies for the equivalent of up to USD30 billion per year, which accounted for half of the bilateral trade between the two countries in 2012. In 2014, Russia and China signed a three-year currency swap deal worth RMB 150 billion (USD 24.5 billion). This was extended for another three years in 2017. In 2015, South Africa and China signed a three-year bilateral swap agreement worth 57 billion rand (USD4.75 billion). Apart from this 2015 agreement, BRICS' bilateral currency swaps have mostly been in the renminbi. This is unsurprising given that the renminbi is the most internationalized of all BRICS' national currencies.

BRICS' efforts toward de-dollarization in international trade have progressed, especially in bilateral trade. Between 2013 and 2019, the use of local currency in India–Russia bilateral trade increased from 6% to 30%. According to Andrey Denisov, the Russian Ambassador to China, about 25% of bilateral trade between Russia and China was settled using local currencies in 2020, which was about a nine-fold growth over less than seven years. In comparison, the use of local currencies in their bilateral trade was about 2–3% during 2013 and 2014. The use of the renminbi in trade in South Africa grew by 65% in 2016. The bilateral currency swaps also proved useful for circumventing US sanctions. Under stringent sanctions in 2014, the bilateral currency swap between Russian and Chinese central banks enabled Russia to circumvent Western isolation and fostered a de-dollarization dynamic between China and Russia. Between October 2015 and March 2016, Russia used these swap lines multiple times to support bilateral trade and direct investment between Russia and China.

At the BRICS country level, Russia has achieved the greatest reduction in the use of the US dollar in its trade since 2013. Russia's trade de-dollarization hit a milestone by the fourth quarter of 2020 when the share of its exports sold in US dollars fell below 50% for the first time. However, the decline of the US dollar was not replaced by the ruble but rather picked up by the euro. The share of euro used in Russia's export transactions increased to 36.1%, contrasting with a mere 8.7% in the first quarter of 2013.

Bilateral trade de-dollarization within BRICS has progressed most rapidly in Russia–China trade. This has been catalyzed by the increasing use of local currencies in Russia's exports to China, especially after major Russian energy companies stopped using the US dollar in their energy exports. For example, in 2015, Gazprom Neft announced that it settled all of its oil exports to China in renminbi. The rise of the euro in Russia–China trade also accelerated in 2019, when Russia's top crude oil producer, Rosneft, switched all export contracts to euros from US dollars to protect itself from intensifying US sanctions. By the end of 2020, more than 83% of Russian exports to China were settled in euros. The euro has now replaced the US dollar and has become the primary vehicle currency in Russia–China trade.

As their relations with the U.S. have both worsened in recent years, Russia and China have moved closer to jointly de-dollarize bilateral trade and promoting the use of local currencies in trade settlements. In 2019, following his meeting with President Xi, Putin confirmed that Russia and China intend to sustain the practice of settlements in national currencies. Both countries signed a joint declaration announcing the elevation of their bilateral relationship to the level of "comprehensive strategic partnership of coordination for a new era". This upgrade in their relationship enables China and Russia to ramp up their collective efforts to reduce dependence on the US dollar, use national currencies in bilateral trade and boost cross-currency settlements by up to 50%. These developments suggest that Russia and China are moving closer to forming a de-dollarization hub as both of their relationships with the U.S. have deteriorated.

Disrupting the Dollar's Dominance in Global Equity Markets

The BRICS stock exchanges alliance is an interesting case of a BRICS coalition mobilized through the market within the existing global financial system. This alliance idea was first suggested by the Hong Kong Exchanges and Clearing Limited (HKEx) in June 2010, shortly after South Africa joined the BRIC group. In October 2011, stock exchanges in BRICS countries announced an initiative to cross-list benchmark equity index derivatives. This initiative brought together Brazil's BM&F BOVESPA, Russia's Moscow Interbank Currency Exchange from Russia, HKEx as the initial China representative, and South Africa's Johannesburg Stock Exchange. The National Stock Exchange of India (NSE) and the BSE Limited (formerly known as the Bombay Stock Exchange) have signed letters of support and will join the alliance after finalizing outstanding requirements.

The BRICS leaders endorsed the formation of this equity market alliance at the 2012 BRICS Summit, and the BRICS stock exchanges alliance also started cross-listing equity benchmark index derivatives that could be bought in local currencies during that summit. Members of the BRICS stock exchanges alliance have planned three stages of implementation for the initiative. The first stage is the cross-listing of benchmark equity index derivatives, which is meant to facilitate liquidity growth in the BRICS markets and strengthen the international position of the BRICS alliance in the global economy. Participating exchanges offer local currency-denominated benchmark equity index derivatives. In the second stage, members of the alliance plan to jointly develop new products for cross-listing on their exchanges. The third stage will include further cooperation in developing joint products and new services.

Although the BRICS stock exchanges alliance was not initiated with the goal of de-dollarization, the outcome is a step toward reducing the US dollar's dominance in the global equities market. At the time of its announcement, the seven participating exchanges represented a combined listed market capitalization of USD9.02 trillion and an equity market trading value per month of USD422 billion, and 9,481 listed companies. They also accounted for over 18% of all exchange-listed derivative contracts traded by volume worldwide at that time. These exchanges collectively represent sizable and fast-growing equity markets that are not traded using the US dollar. Deeper cooperation through cross-listing and joint product development would facilitate the broader use of BRICS local currencies in these equity markets.

A BRICS exchanges alliance is appealing to investors in BRICS countries as well as those overseas. The alliance allows domestic investors within BRICS who want to go offshore to trade index futures and options for each exchange on their domestic market to use their currency, which is free of capital controls or currency risk. For investors outside of the BRICS countries, the alliance offers easy access to major equity index derivatives of the BRICS markets, which gives them an opportunity for portfolio diversification and for gaining exposure to BRICS equity markets. Broader domestic and international participation in the cross-listed financial products will not only raise the profile of the exchanges but also increase the use of BRICS currencies in global equity markets and divert capital traffic away from the dollar-denominated financial assets. Moreover, for investors who already have exposure to BRICS economies, futures are essential for hedging and risk management, which is a necessity for developing a robust financial ecosystem in BRICS countries.

Generally, the "reform-the-status-quo" initiatives have helped BRICS members to reduce their dependence on the US dollar without creating new nondollar institutions or market mechanisms. These initiatives are less effective than "go-it-alone" measures due to the lack of nondollar alternatives. They are likely to be less successful in de-dollarizing the existing global financial system or enabling rising powers to achieve greater autonomy and influence in the global system. However, BRICS group-level initiatives, such as the launch of the CRA as a first line of defense before going to the IMF, and the collective bargaining for SDR reform, have demonstrated a high level of coalitional strength, as BRICS present a united front to the Western-dominated multilateral financial institutions. The sub-BRICS levels' de-dollarization initiatives, such as the unilateral reduction of the share of dollar assets in foreign exchange reserves and the BRICS stock exchanges alliance, directly improve members' autonomy. These measures, however, are of a much smaller scope.

CHAPTER TEN: EVOLUTION OF BRICS AS A DE-DOLLARIZATION COALITION

Generally, the unilateral de-dollarization efforts can't be as effective as that of the coalition, but it points to a possibility that countries can make some independent efforts. For instance, Russia's aggressive reduction in its US dollar asset holdings suggests that for any country subject to US sanctions, it's central bank and sovereign fund can unilaterally de-dollarize its reserve assets as one measure to attempt to weaken the effectiveness of US sanctions. However, in the context of BRICS, it is very unlikely that all BRICS central banks will agree to remove the dollar from their reserves. This is so because the US dollar is still the most widely accepted currency for international settlements, and the US Treasury bond is still the best proxy for risk-free assets. The large dollar asset holdings of some BRICS members prevent them from dumping the US dollar or US Treasury securities on a large scale, as a decrease in US dollar asset value would inevitably incur major losses for these BRICS members. Moreover, the CRA has a limited capacity to provide liquidity needs, and there is also a cap on withdrawals. This means the CRA can only serve as a 'first line of defense' but not a 'lender of last resort' for the BRICS members. Finally, cross-listing among BRICS stock exchanges does not rewrite the rules or standards of global capital markets. If these exchanges want to be attractive to international investors, they must establish regulatory certainty, with convertibility to the US dollar market.

Moreover, compared with the dollar-based equity market, their size and market depth are much smaller. Therefore, at the current stage, BRICS stock exchanges have little capacity to create a large impact on global financial markets.

Moreover, the BRICS alliance requires more negotiations with the incumbent on some aspects of the de-dollarization process. It takes a lot of tact and lobbying for a disruptor to displace an incumbent. Even if there was an opportunity for a BRICS currency to be promoted and to share the dominant currency power position with the US dollar, there is no BRICS currency that could take this responsibility at the moment. As long as the renminbi comes with the strings of capital controls attached, it cannot rise to the dominant currency position either in trade or international finance.

The coalition de-dollarization is different from national or unilateral monetary de-dollarization. It revolves around international negotiation processes that require mutual gains to make the creation of nondollar multilateral institutions and an alternative nondollar infrastructure possible. Even as Russia and other countries most negatively affected by the dollar volatilities would emphasize "go-it-alone" strategies, the strategy can't go far without engaging in intense negotiations. While the pressure from evading the impact of sanctions may motivate the coalition de-dollarization process, there has to be a combination of unilateral and multilateral measures for the de-dollarization effort to achieve the desired level of success.

A key success factor for the BRICS de-dollarization initiative is that the challenge to the US dollar does not only come from US strategic adversaries or competitors but also from US allies and partners in and outside the BRICS coalition who have economic incentives to reduce the dollar's dominance and hedge against exchange risk. Accordingly, it can be argued that bypassing sanctions and geopolitical reasons prompt pivotal states to lead de-dollarization initiatives, but it is the shared economic incentives to reduce currency risks that sustain the de-dollarization coalition in the long term.

Connecting national nondollar financial infrastructures among BRICS can lead to the creation of an alternative nondollar financial system. Also, connecting BRICS-level initiatives with non-Western organizations' initiatives can generate benefits through institutional interactions. The BRICS "go-it-alone" de-dollarization initiatives have to be complemented with sufficient doses of "reform-the-status-quo" initiatives to help create space for the "go-it-alone" measures to act. BRICS has demonstrated a relatively high degree of coalitional strength in the pursuit of "go-it-alone" initiatives as evidenced in the use of the NDB for development finance de-dollarization; the members' commitment to a prospective BRICS alternative to SWIFT; its joint planning for a BRICS digital currency; and the broader BRICS Plus outreach efforts. Although these initiatives remain at a small scale, they create new nondollar mechanisms and help BRICS members achieve greater autonomy. But without adequate commitment to negotiations, the efforts are unlikely to go far.

Although Russia has been the most outspoken and the most active in pursuit of de-dollarization, China is the most capacitated and presents the most credible challenge to the dollar hegemony among the BRICS members. Other members have been less enthusiastic toward de-dollarization, but they have nonetheless participated. The best strategy for the BRICS is not to imagine that a wholesale throw-away of the dollar will ever be achieved. Rather, it is more realistic to accept dollar dominance as a given and seek to nurture and grow alternative institutions, systems, and mechanisms that should initially aim to improve the status quo without significantly attempting to initiate significant changes. The best way for the BRICS coalition to move into leadership is to seek to solve problems that the incumbent overlooked. So, instead of focus on creating alternative financial infrastructure that enables Russia to achieve immunity to US sanctions and access global markets via a nondollar financial system, the BRICS coalition can prioritize using the window of the NDB to source funds for high-return projects in developing countries, which the incumbent is not doing.

It is obvious that the more the US dollar is used for advance sanctions or fear of sanctions the higher the risk of migration to other currencies and other financial systems in the medium-term. Hence, for the BRICS and several other countries that are critical of the U.S. foreign policy the risk of global finance migrating to an alternative financial system is real. While the immediate consequence of this shift is the decline in the US's ability to use sanctions against its strategic adversaries such as Russia, the long-term challenges are immense, as sanction power is a critical tool that strengthens US leadership without the use of military force. Furthermore, it raises questions about the US's ability to advance its political and economic values in the global system and preserve a soft power edge.

Notwithstanding the above considerations, the US dollar is still the dominant currency in nearly every aspect of the current global financial system, and it is unlikely that another currency will replace the dollar any time soon. But from the benefit of history, it is clear that a new alternative dominant currency will join the US dollar and the euro. It can be the yuan if China becomes committed to becoming a more responsible superpower by allowing its currency to float and eliminating the various regimes of capital controls. De-dollarization is not a one-off event but a long-stretched process involving several incremental actions that are founded on well-laid-out policy initiatives that promote nondollar settlements. The process of de-dollarization has been initiated. It is incentivized largely by the abusive use of the US dollar's exorbitant privilege and the stickiness of the mercantilist thinking in the U.S. foreign policy modeling that still considers unfair trade, military domination, and sanctions as useful tools of economic diplomacy; albeit now defunct. As long as the U.S. is glued to the defunct mercantilist, it will continue to abuse the exorbitant privilege, and trying to evade or avoid U.S. sanctions will continue to cause countries to invent and deploy diverse de-dollarization initiatives, individually and as coalitions. The mercantilist doctrine that underlies the U.S. foreign policy thus remains the mythical banana pill that will cause the eventual collapse of the US hegemony. Changing it offers the U.S. the opportunity to remain in a leadership position in the emerging new world order with a growing number of other economic powers.

At the same time, Russia and China can't ride on the heels of the abuse of the US dollar's exorbitant privilege to global leadership; it can't be that so easy. They are still a lot that must be done for them to emerge as trusted leaders in the global financial markets beyond the current success in using their national currencies for group and bilateral trade. Russia will need to check its penchant for territorial expansion to earn the respect of the global community. Very few international investors would want to use the Russian ruble as a reserve currency because of the moral infirmity that Russia carries as a terrorist state; or how else can we describe Russia's penchant for invading other countries and capturing territories in the 21st century? China is fairly much better than Russia in that regard, but its South China Sea bullying, especially wanting to absolve Taiwan that has for decades now remained a country, albeit not so recognized by the UN, is a stain on its moral legitimacy to have its yuan become a major reserve currency staying side-by-side with the U.S. dollar. The small island countries around China should be allowed to exist. Where there is a strong case to absolve them into China, it should be via a democratically conducted referendum where the people are allowed to decide where they want to belong.

The use of new financial technologies (e.g., blockchain, digital currencies, and cloud-based financial infrastructure) can propel the formation of a revisionist de-dollarization coalition and strengthen the credibility of collective mobilization. This should lead to the creation of new market instruments and infrastructure that exclude the incumbent power, serve as global public goods with a broader buy-in, and divert global financial traffic away from an archaic incumbent system.

CHAPTER ELEVEN: A NEW GLOBAL CURRENCY – THE CHALLENGE OF COORDINATION

Theoretically, a global currency issued by the BRICS coalition could be a game changer. It is likely to be less volatile and able to improve trade relations among its members. But its success will depend on the currency's strength, legitimacy, and effective collaboration among BRICS nations. The currency's success depends seriously on how it is received by the global investment community. A reliable and trustworthy alternative to the current system could attract investments to the member nations, but volatility and lack of trust will discourage investments and impede economic growth.

A successful BRICS common currency will inevitably impact world financial markets, potentially causing a redistribution of global currency reserves and affecting the demand for other major currencies like the U.S. dollar, euro, and yen. This shift could also influence U.S. monetary policy, global debt markets, and the overall state of the world economy. But there is no guarantee of success for the BRICS global currency initiative. Given that the economies of the BRICS members will not merge, the diverse economic policies among the member countries will damage the credibility and stability of the BRICS currency. The only realistic possibility for a BRICS global currency to succeed is to peg it to either the U.S. dollar or the euro, otherwise, the currency may lack global legitimacy. The BRICS global currency can't be pegged to the yuan because its global convertibility and acceptability are constrained by the capital controls imposed by the Chinese government. So rather than contemplate a global currency now, the best that the BRICS members can do is to continue trading among themselves using their national currencies until such a time that the yuan, rupee, real, or ruble gain global convertibility to the extent of adopted as the BRICS reference currency.

A BRICS Alternative to the U.S. Dollar is Being Over-ambitious

Predictions about the BRICS countries as the fastest-growing economies are not as much in doubt as the idea that they can create a U.S. dollar alternative. For now, the BRICS alliance is doing very well as a diplomatic forum and development financing coalition outside of the Western mainstream. They will continue to do well in that perspective, perhaps in some sense as representatives of the Global South, and "an alternative model to the G7", serving as an "informal forum" of countries who seek to promote trade among themselves, as much as possible, using their national currencies, growing their equity markets, and perfecting seamless payment/exchange mechanisms among their ranks. Rather than seek to challenge the incumbent or existing models of the World Bank and IMF, the BRICS coalition can work with it and through it to get better bargains for members.

The NDB and CRA are certainly novel ideas and healthy achievements for the BRICS bloc. But it is not expedient to consider them as alternatives to the World Bank and IMF respectively, although it is possible that with time, they become so, then so be it. Equally, the BRICS should not be turned into an anchor point for the expansionistic quests of either Russia or China. For instance, since the start of the Russian war in Ukraine, the BRICS countries have only distanced themselves further from the so-called West. Neither India, Brazil, South Africa, nor China are taking part in sanctions against Russia. Rather we have seen near-historic levels of trade between India and Brazil with Russia. The unintended narrative being created is that the BRICS is a pro-East or anti-West group, and therefore the currency it hopes to create will be a pro-East creation and not necessarily global.

Political scientist Matthew Bishop from the University of Sheffield in an article noted that some Western policymakers worry that the BRICS may become less an economic club of rising powers seeking to influence global growth and development and more a political one defined by their authoritarian nationalism. Maihold of the German Institute for International and Security Affairs observes however that the

BRICS does not qualify to be described as counter-West or pro-East but a forum for increased sovereign and autonomous thought. In a bipolar world, he believes South Africa, India, and Brazil are simply "vying for better terms." China and Russia are on the other hand, using the platform for their global political ambitions, Maihold added, pointing to Beijing's offer to mediate the war in Ukraine and the joint military exercises it held with Russia in South Africa. Maihold believes the West has noticed this change in tact and is trying to counteract it. "They are looking very closely," he said. "At the G7 summit in Germany in 2022, they made a point of inviting South Africa and India, to prevent the optics that the G7 was standing against BRICS."

The BRIC Commodity/Currency Swap Proposal is possible

At the last BRICS summit held in March in New Delhi, development banks of the participating countries agreed on a proposal to extend credit in local currency for trade, project financing, and infrastructure projects. Some financial gurus have dismissed the BRICS agreement as purely symbolic. Yet, the current intra-BRICS trade stands at $307 billion; it is set to reach $500 billion by 2015. Within BRICS, China is the dominant country, exporting $135 billion in goods and services a year to its partners. As trade increases, China could move swiftly to provide renminbi for importers of Chinese goods. At this time, China facilitates payment in renminbi through a central bank liquidity swap. Since 2009, 16 countries have exchanged local currencies for a total of 1.6 trillion renminbi; more are in line to participate—Japan and the UK are rumored to be in the queue. The list will certainly increase because the processes eased the settlement of the trade.

Four factors make a central bank liquidity swap particularly important. First, using the US dollar to intermediate causes a loss of purchasing power as the dollar value rises and it becomes scarce to source. Second, following the 2008 financial crisis, the dollar exchange rate volatility has been on the rise making it difficult to predict the cost of dollars. This puts many countries passing their trading through the dollar in a more difficult situation. Third, there is an opportunity to save on transaction costs when the BRICS countries exchange their currencies directly without passing through the US dollar. It is estimated that BRICS countries save $12.3 billion a year in banking services by transacting directly with their currencies. Lastly, a central bank liquidity swap will benefit small businesses. For instance, drawing on a swap line from China, the Reserve Bank of India (RBI) can offer attractive loans to businesses through the Export-Import Bank in renminbi to finance Chinese deals without having to worry about inadequate dollar supply.

The swap deal is not without its risks. For example, in the late 1950s, India entered into a similar currency agreement with the defunct USSR largely for arms deals. India ran up a trade deficit and from 1955-76, Russia accumulated upwards of $350 million in non-convertible rupees. As a result, Russia sought a strategic advantage from its poorer trading partner. India's signature commodities such as tea were re-exported by Russia to Western markets, shrinking India's market share with key trading partners. Moscow even petitioned for naval base rights. Prime Minister Indira Gandhi refused, believing that the quid pro quo would threaten regional security. As with the USSR then, so is the possibility with China now. Notwithstanding the risks, the BRICS swaps are likely to save money on imports/exports by freeing the members from currency fluctuations and reducing the cost of funds. What is of importance however is how the terms will be decided and whether the major players – China and Russia – are not likely to take advantage of the other members.

Ramp up BRICS Productivity before considering a Global Currency

The U.S. dollar has been the world's primary reserve currency since the 1940s. Under the initial Bretton Woods system, the dollar was pegged to gold and most other currencies were pegged to the dollar. And hence, the dollar became the main intervention or reserve currency. With the collapse of the Bretton Woods system, fluctuations in the dollar's exchange rate, and the rise of other global economic powers, there have been various predictions of the demise of the dollar as the primary reserve currency. Yet, data on the currency composition of reserves indicate that the dollar's share of reserves today is roughly the same as 30 years ago, as is the euro. There have been variations in the dollar's share, but it has never fallen below 50 percent.

The rise of Germany and Japan as major economic powers led to the view that the Deutsche mark and the yen would rival the dollar, dividing the world into three currency blocs. The yen's share of global foreign currency reserves did rise in the 1980s, but peaked at close to 9% in 1991 and since has declined to less than 3%. The Deutsche mark was the main reserve currency among the euro legacy currencies and accounted for the largest share of reserves after the dollar. The share of reserves held in Deutsche marks ranged from 10 to 18% between 1979 and 1998. The decision to establish the European monetary union led to further predictions of the dollar's demise. But currently, the euro is the only other major reserve currency, accounting for one-fourth of foreign currency reserves.

The dollar's role as the primary reserve or global currency evolved organically; it was not established by decree but, rather followed the emergence of the U.S. as the world's major economy and most trusted country in terms of the respect to contracts and the rule of law.

Other reserve currencies will naturally evolve over time

Economists point to several key factors that determine the use of a currency for reserves. These are (1) the size of the domestic economy; (2) the importance of the economy in international trade; (3) the size, depth, and openness of financial markets; (4) the convertibility of the currency; (5) the use of the currency as a currency peg, and (6) the consistency of domestic macroeconomic policies. Considering these factors, the closest alternative to the US dollar at present is the euro. The geopolitical area covered by the euro is only slightly smaller than the U.S. economy, just as the economy of the euro area is only slightly smaller than the U.S. economy. Both the euro area and the U.S. account for a large share of global trade. Both the euro and the dollar are freely convertible, and both economies have a history of sound macroeconomic policies. In addition, the dollar and the euro are the only currencies to which other currencies are regularly pegged. The key factor that may explain the smaller share of the euro as a reserve currency is the size and depth of government bond markets. Although total sovereign debt outstanding in the euro area rivals that of the U.S., there is no common euro area sovereign debt market. This reduces the ease with which holders of euro-denominated securities can buy and sell them, compared with U.S. Treasury securities.

These factors also explain why no emerging market currency accounts for a visible share of global foreign currency reserves. A few emerging markets have become large economies and global trading powers. Likewise, several of the emerging markets have established a history of sound macroeconomic policies resulting in low inflation and sustainable public debt levels. Typically, however, most emerging markets do not have well-developed and open domestic financial markets and globally convertible currencies. This situation will of course change with time, as the emerging markets become more developed and integrated with global capital markets. Financial market development combined with sound macroeconomic policies and open markets will lead to an increased international role for emerging market currencies and a greater diversification of foreign currency reserves. There is a limit to which the BRICS coalition can force that process.

De-dollarization initiatives can't displace the US dollar's global reserve currency status

As long as the U.S. maintains sound macroeconomic policies and deep, liquid, and open financial markets, the dollar will continue to be a major reserve currency. Stronger policy interaction among the BRICS countries may help bring convergence in their real market behavior. Over time, the BRICS may transform into a currency union which will help reduce its intra-regional trade cost and further cement economic integration among them. A BRICS currency union may give its monetary cooperation a transcontinental dimension, making its role more proactive and significant in the promotion of global trade and investment. Such a strategic economic partnership, complementing and strengthening the bilateral and multilateral relations between member states, gives their cooperation a better title and image and will contribute to sustainable and faster economic growth and competitiveness in the global arena. The economies of the BRICS countries may converge to form a geographically distant but economically powerful coalition that takes fuller advantage of their capabilities. But this appears to be how far the BRICS bloc can go now. The BRICS countries need more time to consolidate the progress described above, which is by no means easy. Taking on the challenge of displacing the U.S. dollar can rightly be considered a distraction to the BRICS logical progression course.

For now, the U.S. dollar remains the world's dominant reserve currency, among other such currencies including the euro, the yen, the pound, the renminbi (RMB), the Canadian dollar, the Swiss franc, and the Australian dollar. The dollar has functioned as the world's dominant reserve currency since World War II. Nearly all central banks have to hold a significant portion of their foreign exchange reserves in dollars. About half of the international trade is invoiced in dollars, and about half of all international loans and global debt securities are denominated in dollars. In foreign exchange markets, where currencies are traded, dollars are involved in nearly 90% of all transactions.

Investors consider the U.S. dollar as the preferred fallback currency during major economic crises because its resilience is time-tested. During the global financial crisis of 2008-2009, for example, and amidst the economic turmoil associated with the recent Covid pandemic, investors had to scramble for U.S. dollars believing in its capacity to retain their asset values, and it did. In both recent crises, the U.S. Federal Reserve adopted extraordinary monetary authorities and currency swap lines with other central banks to ease access to dollars.

The U.S. has a responsibility to adjust in line with changing realities

As a country, the U.S. derives direct benefits from the dollar's status as the world's dominant reserve currency. But retaining the benefits comes with a responsibility to use the exorbitant privilege wisely. Many central banks and financial institutions around the world need to hold U.S. dollars and dollar-backed securities like U.S. Treasury bonds, there is strong demand for U.S. dollars. That demand, in turn, allows the U.S. to borrow more cheaply (at lower interest rates) than it would otherwise. The U.S. government, firms, and consumers borrow from foreign creditors in dollars rather than other foreign currencies. As a result, the value of that debt does not depend on fluctuations in exchange rates. When other governments, firms, and individuals borrow in foreign currencies, they incur the risk that swings in exchange rates will cause their real debt level (the size of the debt in the borrower's national currency) to increase, potentially quickly and significantly. U.S. firms and consumers also benefit by saving on transaction costs.

But widespread use of the dollar entails economic risks. Low borrowing costs can lead to the accumulation of debt, and the funds borrowed may not be channeled into productive investments. Additionally, the demand for the dollar associated with its position as a reserve currency can lead to a stronger U.S. dollar. A strong U.S. dollar generally makes it harder for U.S. producers to compete in global markets and can lead to persistent trade deficits, although. U.S. consumers may benefit from less expensive imports. For example, the dollar has strengthened since mid-2021 as the Fed tightened monetary policy to combat rising inflation. In addition to the impact of a rising dollar on U.S. exporters, it will create challenges for many other countries servicing their debts amidst higher interest rates and slowing global economic growth. It is important that, in light of growing disaffection about how the exorbitant privilege is used, the U.S. takes urgent measures to check its foreign military spending and determine to use sanctions more sparingly. Instead of spending on funding wars, the U.S. can refocus on spending on development and building sound relationships with the other major powers to strengthen the effectiveness of its diplomatic outreaches.

CONCLUSION

A preview of the activities of the BRICS coalition shows an active long-run process of de-dollarization, to the effect that the BRICS coalition is playing a significant role in establishing an alternative nondollar system that precipitates broader global de-dollarization. The BRICS' moves are thus in line with the global de-dollarization movement. The US dollar has been the official currency for international trade for years now. However, in recent times there has been talk of creating a new currency in an attempt to dump the dollar and push back against American hegemony.

The de-dollarization movement has received a boost in recent times, especially after the Russia-Ukraine war that started in February 2022. The

BRICS bloc is in the process of creating a new medium for payments that are not founded on or defending either the dollar or euro. The US dollar has enjoyed a powerful status as the global currency since 1944 when it was crowned as global currency. Since then, the US has had a disproportionate amount of influence over other economies. And the powers have helped it to use sanctions as a tool to achieve foreign policy goals. It must be admitted that in many instances the exercise of the US foreign policy goals has helped to stabilize the global policy environment. Many small countries have had their existence and sovereignty preserved thanks to the US. For instance, but for the U.S. intervention, Kuwait would not have been identified as a sovereign country today having been annexed by Iraq in August 1990. In many ways, the U.S. has used its exorbitant privilege to stabilize the world militarily, politically, and economically. However, not all the leaders of countries like the roles played by the U.S. Russia and China particularly would love to see a world with less U.S. influence, and this they seek to achieve by calling a halt to the dollar hegemony. This is the essence of their various de-dollarization initiatives.

The formal argument in support of de-dollarization is that it would reduce other countries' dependence on the US dollar and the US economy, and help mitigate the impact of political economic changes in the US on their economies. Also, countries can reduce their exposure to currency fluctuations and interest rate changes, which can help to improve economic stability and reduce the risk of financial crises. This move has been gaining speed in the last few years. In 2022, the IMF noted that central banks today are not holding the greenback as reserves in the same quantities as yesteryear. The dollar's share of global foreign-exchange reserves fell below 59% in the final quarter of 2022, extending a two-decade decline, according to the IMF's Currency Composition of Official Foreign Exchange Reserves data. Incidentally, the decline in the dollar's share has not been accompanied by an increase in the shares of the pound sterling, yen, and euro, other long-standing reserve currencies. Rather, the shift out of dollars has been in two directions: a quarter into the Chinese renminbi, and three quarters into the currencies of smaller countries that have played a more limited role as reserve currencies, still leaving the U.S. dollar as the most dominant currency unless and until China renders the yuan a free global currency without significant capital controls. Below are pertinent concluding remark

The desperation of Russia for de-dollarization is understandable

To punish Russia for its invasion of Ukraine, Western governments froze $300 billion of its foreign currency reserves in 2022, roughly half the total, and expelled Russian banks from SWIFT. Although many feel the sanctions were justified because Russia's recent craving to recover the defunct USSR territories needs to be tamed, some countries with authoritarian bias fear that such a high level of dollar "weaponization" may reach them someday and have decided to stand on the side of Russia. More countries support de-dollarization because Russia and China are their major trading partners, foreign direct investors, and donors/development partners. There are as well some advanced countries (including U.S. allies) who view the U.S. hegemony as hurtful to the growth of the global economy and would want to see a more liberalized global reserve currency regime. For instance, the UK, Germany, and the United Arab Emirates are among the countries that are currently trading in Indian rupees.

The BRICS coalition needs more time to prepare for a common currency

Theoretically, a common currency will be beneficial to the BRICS countries and the coalition. A digital ruble, rupee, and or renminbi can be selected as the BRICS currency or a neutral currency created. To do so successfully, the BRICS bloc may need to transform to a monetary union. China would certainly have a crucial role to play in the development of a common currency as it would add 1.4 billion participants to the system. The combination of India,

China, Brazil, South Africa, and Russia patronizing a currency can be a strong prompter of its legitimacy. The fact that the BRICS members and others have begun to accept trade settlements and investments in yuan, rupee, and ruble instead of the dollar or euro is indicative of the determination by the BRICS nations to change the dollar-dominated system. If the BRICS can come up with a new currency that they start using to trade among themselves, it will be a step further in the de-dollarization journey. But the question is, are the BRICS members willing to transform the alliance into a monetary union or common market like the EU? Will India, for instance, accept the new BRICS currency, bury its rupees, and subject the internal management of its monetary system to a BRICS currency that will ultimately be influenced significantly by China? This consideration is among the issues that may significantly slow down efforts by the BRICS member countries to have a common currency.

SOURCES

https://www.gzeromedia.com/by-ian-bremmer/the-dollar-is-dead-long-live-the-dollar

https://www.rescue.org/article/how-are-global-systems-failing-behind-years-emergency-watchlist

https://www.orfonline.org/expert-speak/brics-future-in-a-changing-world-order/

https://www.hindustantimes.com/ht-insight/international-affairs/brics-impediments-and-potential-areas-of-cooperation-101682584450915.html

https://www.crypto-news-flash.com/bank-of-america-report-dismisses-brics-yuan-and-crypto-as-viable-alternatives-to-bitcoin-as-the-new-world-currency/

https://en.wikipedia.org/wiki/American_decline

https://www.cfr.org/event/rise-and-fall-great-powers-america-china-and-global-order

https://www.cairn-int.info/article-E_HERM_079_0183--the-practical-paradox-the-brics-as-a-ven.htm

https://www.gisreportsonline.com/r/brics-future/

http://www.ijstr.org/final-print/oct2019/Multilateral-Diplomacy-Role-Of-Brics-In-Altering-The-Discourse-Of-Global-Governance.pdf

https://www.barnesandnoble.com/w/managing-development-disruption-risks-uwem-essia/1142764991